O. HENRY
The Man and His Work

E. Stanley
Turnbull

O. HENRY

THE MAN AND HIS WORK

by
E. HUDSON LONG

Philadelphia
UNIVERSITY OF PENNSYLVANIA PRESS
1949

TO MY FATHER AND MOTHER

Preface

ONE of the most widely read American writers during the first decade of this century, O. Henry continues to find followers at home, while abroad his audience grows larger. His life is as romantic as any story he ever wrote. Yet the facts of his biography need reëxamination. Because of suppressed information, scattered sources, and misconceptions, clarification becomes necessary. New material has come to light; lapse of time, moreover, now enables us to appraise his work with greater surety.

I am indebted to many people for helping me. Mrs. Nellie Rowe Jones of the Greensboro, North Carolina, Public Library generously placed at my disposal the manuscripts in the collection there, including the material assembled by the late C. Alphonso Smith. These manuscripts have been transcribed literally in this study. The work done on O. Henry by Smith, who was his life-long friend and first biographer, must always remain the cornerstone upon which any book on the subject must rest. Another friend of O. Henry, the late Tom Tate of Greensboro, told me his recollections of their boyhood years. Besides advising me about the trial, Professor Hyder E. Rollins of Harvard University kindly furnished me a copy of the transcript of the appeal. Professor Luther W. Courtney of Baylor University gave me valuable facts, and Professors Arthur Hobson Quinn and

Robert E. Spiller of the University of Pennsylvania read my manuscript and made helpful criticisms. Especially do I appreciate the assistance of my colleague, Professor Richmond Croom Beatty, who read, criticized, and corrected my entire manuscript. Another colleague, Mr. Philip Mankin, aided me in reading proof. My greatest indebtedness, however, is to Professor Sculley Bradley of the University of Pennsylvania, under whose guidance this study was undertaken, who directed me to unpublished O. Henryana, and who has aided, advised, and encouraged me at all times. For their assistance I also wish to thank Mrs. Sara Coleman Porter, Miss Fannie E. Ratchford, Mr. R. S. Henry, Mr. C. E. Hillyer, Mr. C. A. Pressler, Mr. F. D. Armstrong, Mr. Campbell MacCulloch, and Mr. E. M. Oettinger. In addition to Mr. Leonard J. Meyberg and Doubleday and Company, Inc., the editors of *American Literature* and Appleton-Century-Crofts, Inc. have permitted me to quote material. To my wife I am indebted for typing my manuscript and helping me in numerous ways.

E.H.L.

Vanderbilt University
Nashville, Tennessee
January 29, 1949

Acknowledgment

All O. Henry manuscript material is reproduced in this book by special permission of the executor of the O. Henry estate, who controls all rights governing its use, and to whom anyone wishing to reprint it must apply.

All quotations from the published works of O. Henry and from C. Alphonso Smith's *O. Henry Biography* are by permission of Doubleday and Company, Inc.

I wish to thank both for their generous coöperation.

E. H. L.

Contents

"He no longer saw a rabble, but his brothers seeking the ideal."

—*Brickdust Row*

Introduction

O. HENRY entered literature through the Sunday supple-
ments and the syndicated magazines. His generation of
short-story writers, largely newspaper-trained, included
Ambrose Bierce, Richard Harding Davis, Stephen Crane,
and Jack London, all producing matter for the moment,
but at times combining imagination with experience to
make literature. The short story dominated the fiction of
that period, but a short story that had radically changed.
Under the influence of the fifteen-cent magazine and the
newspaper it was democratized, with special correspond-
ents, as it were, reporting on life for an ever-widening
audience. For the new reading public, romance was in
order, but romance set against a realistic background
and depicting realistic characters. This was what the man
who read the supplement on Sunday afternoon wanted.

Sensing the new market and already trained in telling
a story, O. Henry entered the field to sell his wares. The
new medium required narrative art: the writer provided
entertainment, usually with new backgrounds or methods. O. Henry gave his readers the latest slang, unusual
characters, sentiment, and humor—sometimes with a
dash of slapstick. Successful, he joined the *New York*

1

World, turning out a story a week in the manner of the reporter sent into the streets to gather material. And there he might have remained, in that borderland between journalism and literature; but his art had deeper roots. Though a journalist by trade, by instinct he was a local-colorist. Blending romance and realism to focus the reader's attention upon the background, he followed the regionalists of the preceding era. The everyday scene furnished his material, and through him New York City revealed itself and its people in their daily struggle for existence, sometimes drab or sunken, but never futile. The O. Henry decade opened the new century, as headlines proclaimed the arrival of automobiles, airplanes, electricity, and motion pictures; yet the nineteenth century lingered on, the hansom cab appearing beside the automobile in O. Henry's fiction. And by way of good measure, he added tales of other sections; his stories of the Southwest, the Old South, and Creole New Orleans are among his most successful narratives.

Although his readers delighted in tricks or verbal coruscations which appear to us cheap or brassy, they were a new reading public of broader social range, an audience for characters new to literature. The author's purpose was twofold: to win popularity and to convey a social picture. O. Henry was attuned to one of the principal movements of his day, for along with the rise of the fifteen-cent magazine had come the muckrake era. S. S. McClure, for whose syndicate he wrote, was engaged in exposing corporations and investigating municipal corruption, a reform movement of which Theodore Roosevelt's "trust-busting" became the practical application in politics. Sympathetic for the underdog and believing in man's ability to better himself, O. Henry approved, and by giving his followers enough sensation and sentiment to satisfy, by using humor to present social problems, was able to develop the themes he regarded seriously.

This, together with his art as local-colorist, his narrative skill and abundant humor, lifted his productions above their medium, capturing a more literary audience. And O. Henry's stories for the ephemeral journals became a set of books. So popular did his method become that the short story was thereby standardized. Handbooks teaching the tricks of narrative art appeared upon the market. Correspondence schools were born, from which aspirants to quick and easy money were urged to try literature. The approach to writing was presented as wholly mechanistic; forgetting O. Henry's talent, teachers of the short story instructed their students in his manner. So well had this manner been established by the original that many imitators did achieve a lucrative market with his methods. Some of the writers coming under this influence, like Edna Ferber, Fannie Hurst, and Irvin S. Cobb, did produce capable stories, but the writers with nothing to say could only repeat the mannerisms. Lacking skill, they overworked the surprise ending and repeated the formula until it became mechanical. From this debasement a reaction naturally set in; blamed for his imitators, O. Henry is only now beginning to emerge as the humorist, craftsman, and social historian that he is.

His career was so brief that it has been likened to the burst of a comet; his swiftly achieved influence and quick success led the unwary to suspect that his writing depended on mere cleverness. No other American writer of the short story, however, possessed such varied experience to draw upon, for this American "Caliph of Bagdad" had lived a life as colorful as any in his fiction. By a devious route he came to New York, from beginnings in what now appears a remote era.

Early Life in North Carolina

O. HENRY, as he himself expressed it, was "born and raised in No'th Ca'lina." Born in Greensboro in Guilford County on September 11, 1862, he was christened William Sidney Porter. (In 1898 he changed the spelling of his middle name to Sydney.) There was nothing unusual about his boyhood, despite the fact that it occurred at a time of dramatic events in the history of the nation.

Its aftermath, however, was stamped forcefully upon his memory. His childhood was spent among the surroundings which furnished the carpetbagger, Albion W. Tourgee, the materials for his widely read novel, *A Fool's Errand*. Moreover, Will heard much about the war and reconstruction from participants who had seen the events they recounted. The older people would recall how the disbanded soldiers from the defeated army of Joseph E. Johnston had straggled wearily through the town, followed subsequently by Union soldiers marching along the streets. From his elders Will learned of the slaves' being set free and of the turmoil that followed. The desperate effort of a defeated people to save at least some remnants of their civilization still lingered in the memories of those who had experienced the terrors of re-

5

construction. Although the boyhood of Will Porter was spent in a period of relative peace, it was still one in which memories of recent turmoil were vivid, a romantic period, close to dramatic catastrophe.

Therefore, despite the peace and quiet which characterized the sleepy little town of Greensboro, there was present the constant feeling of nearness to stirring times. It was not until Will Porter was seventeen that the despised Tourgee left Greensboro, never to return. Tourgee, who was really an honest man, had been elected judge by the votes of the enfranchised slaves. This alone was enough to make him so disliked by the white population that his departure was hailed with joy as symbolizing the end of an era. His exodus impressed Will Porter so much that he drew a cartoon to celebrate the event.[1]

Life itself, however, was simple and placid. The stirring stories of past experiences furnished a romantic contrast to life in the "somnolent little Southern town" in which the young North Carolinian spent his first years. Greensboro, like the small city of Weymouth in "The Guardian of the Accolade," was a "dreamy and umbrageous" place, lying "among the low foothills along the brow of a Southern valley." There one saw counterparts of the "old, old square-porticoed mansion, with the wry window-shutters and the paint peeling off in discolored flakes," which was the home of Governor Pemberton of "The Emancipation of Billy," or "the red brick, white-porticoed mansion" which was the Weymouth homestead in "The Guardian of the Accolade."

Along the streets one could have encountered Uncle Bushrod of the latter story on his way to his duties in the bank, that old Negro whose soul was "white as the un-inked pages of the bank ledgers." The click of Governor Pemberton's gold-headed cane may have sounded upon the "rugged brick sidewalk" as the old gentleman in his plug hat emerged through the gate of his "rickety paling-fence." There in the cross street the observer perhaps noticed "several farmers' wagons and a peddler's cart or two," and by chance some "hay wagons and the sprinkling cart" were in evidence. Then, entering the avenue the visitor strolled past the bank, the hotel, the opera house, and the drugstore. The streets were wide and shaded, and as one turned from the business district he found himself in the quiet residential section where the home of Dr. Porter might have passed unnoticed. It was not an antebellum mansion, but a simple, comfortable place, much like its neighbors.

Will Porter came from a well-established family. His maternal grandmother, Abia Shirley, was the daughter of Daniel Shirley, a wealthy planter of Princess Anne County, Virginia, who was a lineal descendant of Sir Robert Shirley of Wiston. As the Shirleys had been staunch royalists at the time of the civil wars in England, the widow of Sir Robert had been the recipient of a letter of gratitude and condolence from King Charles II, lamenting "the greate loss that you and I have sustained. . . ."[2] "King" Carter, aristocratic and baronial Virginia planter, named in honor of the Shirley family one of the manors that he built for his children. At this "Shirley" was born Ann Hill Carter, who became the wife of Light Horse Harry Lee and the mother of Robert E. Lee.

Abia Shirley was married to William Swaim, a Quaker, whose ancestors had emigrated from Holland to New York. At least ten years before the Revolutionary War the Swaim family had moved to North Carolina. This grandfather of Will Porter, who in 1827 became editor of the Greensboro *Patriot*, appears to be the only writer among O. Henry's ancestors. In addition to his journalistic ability, William Swaim possessed courage. During his editorship of the *Patriot* he was approached by certain influential citizens who sought to force him to print their sentiments in his paper. Swaim replied in an editorial: "They soon learned from our tone that we would sooner beg for bread and be free than to compromise our principles for a seat upon a tawdry throne of corruption."[3] Like Thomas Jefferson a strong advocate of abolition, Editor Swaim persistently pointed out the evils inherent in the system of slavery. This attitude naturally brought him hatred and abuse, but he did not move from his position. Besides the resolution of character which appears in his writings, William Swaim possessed a keen and telling wit. When subscribers disappeared, leaving the editor "the bag to hold," he published "a list of the gentlemen," telling how much each one owed, and offered, if any of the delinquents paid the amount due, to "publicly acknowledge the receipt and restore him who sends it to better credit than an act of the legislature could possibly give." At the end of one such delinquent list appears, "Joseph Bryan, whipt anyhow and may be hung. Six dollars."[4]

If Will Porter derived his wit and his gift of expression from his mother's side of the house, it was from his father's people that he received his interest in pharmacy and his wanderlust. This latter quality, however, did not come from his paternal grandmother, Ruth Worth, who was made of sterner stuff. Hard-working and practical, she believed in strict moral conduct. Her brother Jonathan had been governor of North Carolina, and she herself was able to take charge of affairs. She did not flinch when left a widow with seven children and a mortgaged home, but devoted herself to the task before her, maintaining her household with never-failing energy. This grandmother Will Porter knew well. As she grew older and less active, however, her youthful virtues were unhappily obscured. Her appearance and habits, such as taking snuff and smoking a pipe, were not such as to invite the affection of a sensitive child.[5]

Ruth Worth's husband, Sidney Porter, was a clockmaker who migrated from Connecticut to North Carolina. Sidney Porter not only bequeathed to his grandson his name but an enduring desire for the venturous. O. Henry's love of romance and his continual seeking for "what's around the corner" were in the spirit of his paternal grandfather. Sidney Porter, a good-humored man, laughed and joked while he worked, and was beloved by the children. When he opened a general repair shop in Greensboro, his neighbors liked his genial qualities, but his business did not prosper. Pleasant memories persist of a jolly man, who sang while he played the guitar, told funny stories, drew cartoons, and had a habit of frequent tippling.[6]

Will's mother attended what is now the Greensboro College for Women, where she specialized first in French and later in painting and drawing. Like her son, Mary Jane Virginia Swaim enjoyed filling her schoolbooks with interesting sketches. These caught the attention of her classmates, who soon discovered that in addition to talent in drawing, Mary Jane possessed a clever gift for writing essays. A number of her friends found her generous in giving aid with their graduation compositions. Her own graduation essay, which was a prophetic commentary on O. Henry, was "The Influence of Misfortune on the Gifted." Along with the ability to draw pictures and to write, she possessed a good-natured wit and a gift for repartee. A letter written at the age of fifteen reveals the ability to give an unexpected turn to a current saying: "Sherwood you know always does keep a 'stiff upper lip' for he rarely if ever shaves, only when he is in the neighborhood of Miss Betsy or Miss Martha, or Miss Maria or a dozen of Misses at whom he casts sheep's eyes."[7] Unfortunately Will's mother died when he was only three years old and she herself but thirty. It appears that in the Porter home the refining influences had been largely furnished by the mother, whose early death left him in the care of his father and his father's relatives.

Although Will's father, Dr. Algernon Sidney Porter, had once given promise of developing into a physician of repute, his early hopes did not materialize. As he grew older, Dr. Porter gave less attention to his profession and increasingly devoted his time to impracticable inventions. Irresponsible with money, he allowed it to flow through his fingers. He did not bother to collect from his patients but, kind-hearted and generous with people in distress, lent a sympathetic ear to many who took advantage of it. Meanwhile, like some Colonel Beriah Sellers turned mechanic, he went optimistically from one device to another. Believing that he had solved the problem of perpetual motion, the doctor sought to invent a water wheel to run on that principle. A flying machine and a carriage to be run by steam were later ideas which absorbed his mind and drained his energies.[8] The neglected medical practice began to dwindle; rumors circulated, and it was whispered about that Dr. Porter was no longer a capable physician. Eventually the practice declined to almost nothing, and Dr. Porter ceased to be a support for the family.[9]

The burden of maintaining the household fell upon the shoulders of his sister, Lina Porter, an exceptional woman whose influence upon Will was both deep and lasting. To earn a living she set up a schoolroom in a small building on the Porter premises. An able teacher, she won the affection of her pupils, among them John H. Dillard, who later declared her the "greatest influence in his life, a lover of truth and beauty."[10] She enjoyed books, especially poetry, and read aloud well, quoting frequently from the verses of Father Ryan. Other favorite authors were Dickens and Scott, and she read them often.

Miss Lina's love for books, however, was but one aspect of her nature. While she inculcated an appreciation of good literature, this teacher was capable of sudden spells of anger. She frequently gave vent to gusty outbursts of profanity, and on one occasion downed a fleeing pupil with a well-aimed brickbat.[11] O. Henry's picture of Miss Azalea Adair in "A Municipal Report" was certainly not based on his maiden aunt. Far from being the gentle, retiring lady of the Southern tradition, Miss Lina was perfectly able to take care of herself. With a violent temper and a puritanical nature, Miss Lina often appeared harsh to Will and his brother, and since it was she who was really in charge of the Porter household, the home life of the family was molded by her character. Moreover, she was too preoccupied with schoolteaching to keep the house in order; Dr. Porter's room was littered with wooden wheels and all sorts of mechanical gadgets constantly escaping from the pile under the bed. During the years of 1879 and '80, Bettie Caldwell, who was a paying guest in the home, found it silent and unhappy. While Miss Caldwell remained, the family did not sit down to a meal together. Dr. Porter and his mother always ate together, but the others ate separately.[12]

Although Will was silent on the subject, it was nevertheless easy for his playmates to discern his embarrassment. Tom Tate, a neighbor and a student of Miss Lina's, was a constant playmate of Will's and frequently visited the house. Tom recalled Dr. Porter's inventions, the junk that cluttered the place, and "Grandma" Porter dipping snuff and smoking a pipe.[13] Later in life Will Porter confided to Mrs. Dick Hall that his childhood at home had been unhappy. There was a lack of understanding between them, which led Will to suppose that Miss Lina regarded him as a nuisance.[14] Actually Miss Lina was fond of her nephew, who was a favorite pupil at her school. It was only natural that she should be anxious that Will and his brother become self-supporting.

But Will was compensated with other happy boyhood experiences. No matter how harsh or violent in temper Miss Lina might be, she knew how to make schoolwork interesting, and she was quick to perceive the boy's interest in his studies and his genuine appreciation of literature. Her method of teaching was such as to impart a lifelong love of books. She did not teach the history of literature, but the spirit; she knew how to bring literature to life, and those pupils who caught her enthusiasm found reading a pleasure. Sometimes she would read to them in the evenings, and on special occasions the youngsters would roast chestnuts, pop corn, and then follow the feasting with a storytelling period, in which each pupil participated in turn. Here Will excelled, and the others anticipated hearing his contribution, which was always original and exciting. Will also possessed another talent which delighted his companions: he was developing the ability to draw. Boyhood friends recalled how Will could work a sum on the blackboard with one hand, while with the other he caricatured Miss Lina, alertly erasing his drawing before she could turn around.[15] Will remained in school until he was fifteen, and seems to have been a general favorite.

His inventive skill in devising new games contributed to his popularity. In an English magazine Will discovered two serial stories which he followed avidly. From these adventure yarns, "Jack Harkaway" and "Dick Lightheart," he derived the idea of dividing Miss Lina's pupils into contesting groups. Two clubs were formed, the Brick-bats and the Union Jacks. The respective members established headquarters filled with wooden battle-axes, spears, old cavalry sabers, and homemade armor improvised from whatever came to hand. Will Porter became an enthusiastic member of the Union Jacks, who located their armory in a vacant building of the old Edgeworth Seminary. Meetings at which the boys planned raids and readied their weapons were held nightly. As far as limited facilities would permit, the Union Jacks observed the forms of knighthood, and titles were bestowed upon the worthy, in romantic tradition. After the rituals of a meeting had been performed, the band set forth in quest of adventure. Perchance the venture led to inglorious retreat, for if a ghost appeared—ghosts were to be seen in those days in the South—shields and swords were discarded, while the knights-errant abruptly took to their heels in the opposite direction.[16]

The boys often hiked to the old Guilford battleground and spent hours looking for relics. If some lucky searcher unearthed a piece of shell or a rusty old sword blade, the jubilant boys hastened home to display their treasure. Will knew every spot of the battlefield, for he was as keenly interested in searching for these rusty implements of war as he was later to be in seeking buried treasure in Texas.

With his boyhood chum, Tom Tate, Will played other games, such as Indian or Ku Klux Klan.[17] The Indian game provided plenty of excitement for the opposing redskins were impersonated by Mr. Tate's hogs. Will and Tom sometimes spent hours chasing an arrow-smitten hog to remove the evidence of their marksmanship before Mr. Tate came home. Miss Lina often entertained Will and Tom by taking them for walks, and one warm day she suggested going wading. The barelegged boys quickly waded out into the shallow water, splashing and shouting, while Miss Lina walked in, holding her skirts above her knees to avoid wetting them. Suddenly sensing that something was amiss, she began to peer around. Her gaze discovered a male resident of Greensboro, peeping at her between the branches of a bush. When the mere sight of a stocking was considered shocking, a lady in wading was a rare spectacle, but loosing upon the unfortunate beholder a withering stream of invective, followed by a broadside of profanity, she sent him scurrying. Miss Lina knew how to take care of herself; no sheltered type was she.[18]

As Will grew older, he participated in the camping, fishing, and serenading that were pastimes of the community. Serenading was especially great fun, for he possessed a good voice and knew how to strum the guitar. Moreover it offered the opportunity of strolling over to see Sallie Coleman in the evening when the April moon was shining. Sitting on the edge of the porch, he would lean his head back against the honeysuckle until Sallie went inside and brought out the guitar. He later said, ". . . pretty soon all of us would be singing the 'Swanee River' and 'In the Evening by the Moonlight.' "[19] There were other times when groups of boys went around the town, serenading the young ladies after they had retired, and in these parties Will and his guitar usually took part.

What seems to have given him more pleasure than anything else, however, were long walks with a friend. He and Tom Tate often spent a whole afternoon out-of-doors reading and talking, and it was during this period of his life that Will did most of his reading. The *Arabian Nights* and Burton's *Anatomy of Melancholy* were his favorite classics, both of which left a definite impression that he never outgrew. Although like most young boys he had a predilection for the dime novel, the greater part of his reading was good. The books he read, together with the stories told him by Miss Lina, later had much to do with shaping his career as a writer.

It was Tom Tate who furnished the material which C. Alphonso Smith used in his biography for his study

of O. Henry's reading.[20] Tom and Will had kindred
tastes and did much of their reading together. Among
their favorite authors were Scott, Dickens, Thackeray,
Reade, Wilkie Collins, Hugo, and Dumas. Dickens' unfinished novel, *The Mystery of Edwin Drood,* fascinated
Will; he read it several times and made a number of unsuccessful attempts to complete the story. An early interest in Jane Porter's *The Scottish Chiefs* had led him to
read Scott. He considered *Bleak House* the best of Dickens' works, while he acclaimed *Vanity Fair* as the best of
Thackeray. He was particularly enthusiastic over Charles
Reade's *The Cloister and the Hearth,* which he praised by
saying, "I never saw such a novel. There is material there
for dozens of short stories in that one book alone." Another favorite was John Esten Cooke's *Surry of Eagle's
Nest,* which Will and Tom admired because of its charac-
terizations of Jeb Stuart and Stonewall Jackson, the Con-
federate heroes who had most inflamed their imagina-
tions. Among the dime novels the boys devoured were the
"Ten Cent Novels" of George Munro, which included
such titles as *The Red Rover, The Wood Demon,* and *The
Terror of Jamaica.* Another early interest was the super-
natural story, but Samuel Warren's novel *Ten Thousand
a Year* made a deeper impression. Will thought Warren's
character of Oily Gammon the best portrait of a villain
he had met, and he afterwards called one of the local
lawyers by that name.[21]

There were other pleasures than reading, however, and

when the boys grew older they began to travel to other parts of the state. An extended camping trip once took them through a number of small towns. Will was as absorbed in the character of each as he was later to be in New York, and with keen interest recalled vividly characteristics of the communities and their inhabitants which had been unnoticed by the other boys.[22] Camping and fishing he enjoyed, but what he liked better was to wander without a set purpose, observing places and people.

As Dr. Porter had gradually ceased to practice, and Miss Lina was hard pressed to support the family, Will realized that he must forego further education and take the first job that offered. When his Uncle Clark suggested that his nephew become a clerk in his drugstore, Will accepted. Located on Elm Street across from the old Benbow Hotel, the store was a social gathering place for residents of the neighborhood. Many of the local celebrities met daily in the drugstore, where they repeated the news, exchanged stories, talked politics, or refought the Civil War while they played checkers or dominoes. These patrons and loungers were a curious study in character types of the Old South; in his spare time Will amused himself by drawing caricatures of them. They appealed to his sense of the ludicrous, while their narrow and prejudiced observations developed his distaste for what he termed the "professional Southerner."

In a short time these drawings earned him a reputation as a humorist. Knowing how to seize upon a peculiar characteristic and reproduce it with a few deft strokes, he could portray anyone. When somebody he did not know asked for credit or paid a bill during Clark Porter's absence, Will drew a sketch of him, so vividly that his uncle never failed to recognize the person. In the drawings he made of groups Will came close to social history in depicting the life of the community. Each picture contained a central theme, illustrated by a few essential delineations, excluding all unnecessary details—a method he later employed so successfully through the medium of the short story.[23] Many of these sketches are today preserved in the Greensboro Public Library and in the hotel which bears his name. During his five years in the drugstore his reputation as an artist grew, and he was offered the opportunity of free instruction at a school in Mebane, North Carolina, an advantage he refused because of lack of money for the necessary clothes and books.[24]

Amusing as this life of cartooning and conversation may have been, Will became dissatisfied. As C. Alphonso Smith observed, "No profession attracted him, and there was no one in Greensboro doing anything that O. Henry would have liked to do permanently."[25] The drugstore appeared to offer nothing but stagnation, and there seemed to be no prospect of finding a better position. Will was both sensitive and proud. Knowing that everyone with whom he associated was familiar with the decline of his father's fortunes and the dilapidation of his home, he became even more shy and retiring. No doubt he was already looking around for a chance to escape from both it and his job when an unexpected circumstance gave him the opportunity.

As the practice of Dr. Porter dwindled away, most of it fell to another Greensboro physician, Dr. James K. Hall. Young Porter had filled many a prescription for him, and the two became very good friends. Dr. Hall was familiar with the Porter household and worried about the cough which Will seemed unable to overcome. One day he came to the boy with a welcome suggestion. Three sons of the Doctor had gone to Texas to seek their fortunes, and one of them, Lee Hall, had become a captain in the Texas Rangers. The Captain's fame had reached back to his native town, where news of his exploits were always received with interest, for "Red" Hall, as he was familiarly known, had assumed the proportions of a hero. Dr. and Mrs. Hall were planning to make a visit to their sons in Texas, and Dr. Hall suggested that Will accompany them. The change would be good for him; he could get out of the drugstore and into the open air, where he would have a chance to get rid of his cough.[26]

Will was quick to agree. The prospect was alluring: the glamour of the famous Ranger Captain, the romance of new and faraway places and possible battles with outlaws and rustlers, the end of his confinement in the drugstore, a healthful climate, and freedom to do as he pleased. No longer would Aunt Lina or Grandma Ruth be able to interfere with him. Free from all family embarrassment, he would be able to stand on his own feet in a new land. One day in March 1882 a train pulled out of Greensboro, Texas-bound. On it were Dr. and Mrs. Hall, accompanied by young William Sidney Porter, intent upon seeking his fortune on a faraway ranch by the Rio Grande.

～ III ～

Ranch Days in Texas

ALTHOUGH the journey from Greensboro to Texas was
long and tiresome, Will Porter, not quite twenty years
old, enjoyed it. To reach Cotulla in 1882, one had to
spend at least ninety-five hours on the train, and the
journey entailed the use of several railroads.[1] To Will
the many stopovers afforded a welcome glimpse of new
and strange cities. He changed trains at Charlotte, left
his native state for the first time, and went on to Atlanta,
where another change was made. Since few people traveled as much as a thousand miles in the eighties, the cars
were poorly equipped. Frequently passengers were
forced to go for hours without drinking water, while the
train lay at a siding in the blistering heat or crept along
the bumpy tracks. As changes or layovers often necessi-
tated overnight stops, Will must have been five or six days
en route, yet the passengers did not seem to mind delays
and sometimes requested the conductor to stop the train
to allow the ladies to pick flowers. Writing to Mrs. Hall
on March 13, 1884, Will jokingly said, "You remember
how often you used to have the train stopped to gather
verbenas when you were coming out here." In a portion

of this same letter which was deleted by Smith, Will wrote:

I can go over in my mind almost every little incident in our trip to this country. I can see the conductor walking towards me with Dr. Hall's bottle of currant wine in his hands, which he let roll away from him down the centre of the car some 300 times on the journey, and which the conductor invariably brought to me, handing it in full sight of everybody, and saying, "Here young man here's your bottle." I think he always suspected the Dr. of dropping it but when he passed along by his seat with it, the Dr. would survey the bottle with such an indifferent, unrecognizing look that he always settled on me as the guilty party.[2]

In spite of the delays caused by the flower-gathering ladies, the party finally arrived in Houston, where they again changed trains and were met by some old friends of the Doctor's. The Cave family, knowing that Dr. Hall and his party were passing through, were on hand to greet them.[3] At this brief meeting Will became attracted to Lollie Cave and promised to pay her family a visit when ranch life permitted. Later they became good friends. From Houston, Will and his party continued through San Antonio, and then to Cotulla, where they were probably conveyed to the ranch in the manner described by O. Henry in "Hygeia at the Solito":

At Rincon, a hundred miles from San Antonio, they left the train for a buckboard which was waiting there for Raidler. In this they travelled the thirty miles between the station and their destination. . . . They sped upon velvet wheels across an exhilarant savanna. The pair of Spanish ponies struck a nimble, tireless trot, which gait they occasionally relieved by a wild, untrammelled gallop. The air was wine and seltzer, perfumed, as they absorbed it, with the delicate redolence of prairie flowers. The road perished, and the buckboard swam the unchartered billows of the grass itself, steered by the practiced hand of Raidler, to whom each tiny distant mott of trees was a signboard, each convolution of the low hills a voucher of course and distance.[4]

So it must have seemed to Will Porter at the time of his first journey from the station at Cotulla to the ranch. At the ranch itself there was not much to see, for Lee Hall had been too much absorbed in other matters to have time for housebuilding. The first house occupied by the Captain and his bride was a small frame dwelling of one room, about twelve feet long and eight feet wide. Another was soon built, however, which consisted of two rooms with a wide gallery across the front in the typical style of the Texas ranch house. Built of logs and adobe, with a guncase stacked with loaded rifles and revolvers displayed on the gallery, the house bespoke the character of the occupants. They lived in the open, and if the houses were small, there was compensation in the vast extent of the ranch itself. Although most of it was in La Salle County, where the cattle could be watered by the Nueces River, it extended into McMullen County and into Frio, where the river of that name joined the Nueces. Because of the limited rainfall in McMullen County, there were few settlers. Its thick brush, however, made an excellent covert, which turned it into a refuge for outlaws, not only from the rest of Texas but also from Mexico. According to Dora Neill Raymond, the ranch in 1881 stretched over about 250,000 acres, and in April 1883, a correspondent of the *Corpus Christi Caller* estimated that it contained 400,000 acres. Dr. Raymond has reckoned its circuit at 120 miles, within which were pastured about 12,000 head of cattle and 6,000 sheep.[5] Old-time Texans did not count mustangs, which were native to the prairie. The cattle, of course, were Texas longhorns.

Will Porter's first impressions were those natural to a person reared in the Old South and then suddenly transported to the rolling prairies of the Southwest, where everything was new and strange. The climate, manners, and customs of the country intrigued him, but most of all his interest centered on Captain Lee Hall. It was in 1880, according to J. Frank Dobie, that Red Hall resigned from the ranger service to take charge of the Dull Ranch, which belonged to the Dull brothers of Harrisburg, Pennsylvania.[6] Captain Hall, while operating the ranch as superintendent, continued to live an eventful and dangerous life. Because of constant threats of death, he usually traveled at night with cocked six-shooters. Lee Hall was one of the outstanding men of the frontier. One of his many achievements, the breaking up of notorious gangs of outlaws, contributed much toward making southwest Texas a safer community to live in. It was at this period, during the war between the ranchmen and the cattle thieves, that Will Porter saw something of the real desperado. From Lee Hall he learned about the outlaw, the ranger, the Mexican sheep herder, and the cowboy troubadour—all of whom were to figure in his stories of the Southwest. Under the guidance of the Ranger captain he became acquainted with the plains and the chaparral. He could have had no better mentor.

The nearest town was Cotulla, where the I. & G. N. stopped to load its freight cars with wool or cattle. Occasionally a passenger alighted there or boarded the train, from the window of which one could see a few Mexicans lounging before the small pine building which passed for a hotel, a clump of mesquite trees, some stray dogs, and a saloon. This saloon, which was the central spot of the town, served as gathering place for the surrounding countryside. Beyond the swinging doors were the tables where the cowboys and ranchmen played poker or monte, while the whiskey bottles passed along the bar and the clink of silver dollars broke through the noise of voices. Cotulla was another world from the "somnolent little Southern town" of Greensboro.

Although Will saw much of Lee Hall, the family with whom he actually lived on the ranch was that of Lee's brother Dick, whose task it was to look after the sheep ranch, where the accommodations were of the most primitive sort. The frame house which was the original ranch structure sheltered Dick Hall, his wife, their infant daughter, Mrs. Hall's brother, B. F. Hughes, and now Will Porter. It had been changed to meet the increasing demands of the occupants, but it was far from adequate. Hyder E. Rollins described it thus: "It was composed of

two small rooms, one the bedroom of Mrs. Hall, the
other divided by a curtain into a kitchen and dining
room. The three men slept in the open air throughout the
year."[7] No one seems to have objected to this arrange-
ment, for Will makes no mention of being uncomfortable.
This family had a marked influence upon Will's development. While Dick Hall and Hughes educated him in the
curriculum of the sheep ranch, Mrs. Hall sought to interest him in her books. The results were gratifying on
both counts. Will learned about sheep and his delight
in reading was rekindled. Mrs. Dick Hall, a native of
Texas, had been educated in Virginia and Louisiana.
Offering Will her books, she carried on the formation of
his literary taste already begun by Aunt Lina back in
Greensboro.

This was an environment in which Will could not help
learning all sorts of things. He was keenly interested in
the cowboys who worked on the ranch, and he wished to
become one himself. Sheep were all right for fresh air
and exercise, but it was the cowboy with six-shooter and
chaps who caught his imagination.

Among the cowboys on the Dull Ranch were several
who had won fame while serving under Captain Hall in
his Ranger company.[8] One of them, Cavin, had been an
excellent scout in Hall's old command and was employed
as ranch pilot. Using the stars for his guide, Cavin took
short cuts across the ranch, going from place to place at
night as he pleased. Sam Platt was there along with
Charlie McKinney, who had ridden with Hall in 1879.

Netteville Devine had gone on the hunt for the outlaw Sam Bass, who shot it out with the Rangers at Round Rock. Also in the group was Will Hall, the Captain's younger brother, and another brother, Frank, who acted as cowpuncher and sometimes aided Dick in looking after the sheep ranch. Dick Hall, it should be noted, was quite capable of more than tending sheep; with Devine he had been one of the posse sent to capture Sam Bass. Association with such men was interesting to Will, for all of them, even those he had known back home, were changed by the life of the range. Ed Brockman, another North Carolinian, who like Will had come to the ranch in search of adventure and opportunity, had been assigned to the commissary tent. Lee Hall had too many trusted hands to take chances with greenhorns: Ed Brockman and Will Porter would have to earn their spurs.

Anxious to have the cowboys accept him as an equal, Will determined to familiarize himself at once with their work and their ways. Living the same life that the others on the ranch did, he persevered until finally the cowboys were ready to accept him. Hyder E. Rollins tells us that Porter learned to ride and rope, and that, according to Hughes, he developed into a "regular bronco-buster."[9] Porter himself in later life told Mabel Wagnalls that he had been a Texas cowboy.[10] Moreover, we have the further authority of Mrs. Lee Hall that Will "acted as a cowboy for a period under Captain Hall about the year 1882."[11] Will became on friendly and then intimate terms with the men, who gladly helped him to advance step by step. When they felt that he needed taking down a peg, they punished him in their own way by silence and absolute politeness. Finally the time came when Will Porter received the "punchers' accolade." Yelling at the top of their lungs, the cowboys with six-shooters blazing startled him from slumber as one of them dragging a saddle galloped wildly across his bed. When Will protested, they stretched him over a roll of blankets and thrashed him with leather leggings. An hour later they let him go. After that he was one of them.[12]

O. Henry's Western stories testify to his intimate knowledge of the cattle country and of those who participated in its drama. Davis and Maurice have claimed that Porter was an expert marksman. Occasionally in his New York days he allowed some of his friends to see him perform at the shooting gallery, where all of them were impressed with his marksmanship.[13] Although Al Jennings declared that Porter seemed to be afraid of a gun, handling it as though it were "a live scorpion," there is no real contradiction.[14] Jennings and Porter's New York associates looked at marksmanship from entirely different angles.

Once Will Porter had proved to himself that he could hold his own in the cow camps, he began to relax into his natural disposition for idleness. Stretched out on a canvas cot shaded by hackberry trees, he strummed a guitar while he learned the songs of the Mexican sheep herders. Although he admired the cowboys, he preferred to spend his time in his own way. Instead of herding sheep or rid-

ing after cattle he now found more pleasure in the study
of languages. Here on the Dull Ranch Will took up un-
aided the reading of French and German.[15] Making an
effort alone to study these languages was too much for
him to continue, however, and there is only a smattering
of French reflected in his stories or correspondence, and
practically no German. With Spanish, on the other hand,
he was more successful. Turning his attention from
French and German to that language, he acquired a fair
knowledge which is evidenced in his stories of the Southwest and Latin America.

Most of the cowboys spoke a brand of Spanish acquired from the Mexican ranch hands, a mixture of
Spanish, English, and Mexican dialect known to Texans
as "Greaser." Buying a Spanish grammar, Porter was
soon able to speak and write a correct form of the language, and he mastered the "Greaser" dialect with avid-
ity. He learned not only quickly but well, for within three
months he was acclaimed "the best speaker of Spanish on
the ranch."[16] Will modestly said at the time, "I am with
Spanish like Doctor Hall's patients, still 'progressing,'
and can now tell a Mexican in the highest and most
grammatical Castilian to tie a horse without his thinking
I mean for him to turn him loose." In the same vein he
added, "I have been known to give directions about a
road in such a scientific and idiomatic manner that a
large outfit of the descendants of the Montezumas have
lost themselves in less than thirty minutes."[17]

While devoting himself to learning Spanish he also

turned his attention to the study of his native tongue. Webster's Dictionary became his constant companion, and he perused it diligently. It was at this period that he laid the foundation of the fastidious and accurate vocabulary that was later to delight readers and astound the critics. Soon his proficiency was so great that he could challenge his associates for a word that he could not spell or define. Legend has it that he was never stumped.[18] He read the dictionary as others read fiction. More than a reference book to him, it became a source of ideas, a word-hoard to be opened in reality. With Mrs. Hall he discussed the difference between the Webster Dictionary and Worcester's, commenting on the differences of spelling and pronunciation, which he knew by heart. Mrs. Hall, who advocated Worcester, had no chance against this well-armed champion of Webster.

She regarded Will's thirst for knowledge as unquenchable and marveled at the way he devoured the books which she had brought to the ranch with her. Her library was well stocked with classics and history, which Will read with keen interest. Apparently he relished everything—history, fiction, biography, science, and poetry;[19] he not only read the books but talked about them eagerly. Tennyson became his favorite poet and remained so until the end. When he quoted Tennyson to Mrs. Dick Hall or talked with her about Dickens she was delighted. Her library was sometimes augmented by orders from Austin and San Antonio, for Mrs. Lee Hall liked to read also, and the two of them tried to keep informed on current books. Porter was fortunate in knowing two such women. Mrs. Lee Hall, a Pennsylvanian, brought an influence of the East into the bare and somewhat wild existence. Together the two women kept before him the contrast between the ranch life and the culture of the older states.

Naturally he found Texas lacking in much to which he had been accustomed in Greensboro, and in his letters back home he commented on the differences. In one of his letters to Mrs. J. K. Hall he said:

In your letter be certain to refer as much as possible to the advantages of civilized life over the barbarous; you might mention the theatres you see there, the nice things you eat, warm fires, niggers to cook and bring in wood; a special reference to nice beefsteak would be advisable. You know our being reminded of these luxuries makes us contented and happy. When we hear of you people at home eating turkeys and mince pies and getting drunk Christmas and having a fine time generally we become more and more reconciled to this country and would not leave it for anything. . . .

You ought by all means to come back to Texas this winter; you would love it more and more; that same little breeze you looked for so anxiously last summer is with us now, as cold as Callum Brothers suppose their soda water to be.[20]

On December 8, 1883, Will wrote a letter to Dr. W. P. Beall, a Greensboro physician, in which he enclosed a drama written on foolscap paper. A burlesque about the citizens of Greensboro, it was to be read aloud in the drugstore by the doctor. Will sent pictures along with it, including one of the doctor with the following Limerick:

A good-natured young doctor named Beall
Was quite pleased when his patients got well
 When they didn't do so
 He would blame the drug-sto'
And say, "Drugs is now made for to sell."

On the blank space of paper which had been left at the end of the drama Will wrote the following parody of "The Bells":

The Dudes

See the City's lovely dudes—,
Sidewalk dudes—,
What a world of broken hearts
Their promenade preludes.
Clerks and students of the law
Beauties all without a flaw
Let us all get off the sidewalk for the dudes
For the dudes, dudes, dudes,
Dudes, dudes, dudes;
For the lady killing, fascinating dudes.

Look up there all in a row!
Gallery dudes—
With what grace they assume all
Such enticing attitudes,
With their eyes, eyes, eyes,
And their sentimental sighs,
Oh full rare and fragrant flowers are the dudes
Are the dudes, dudes, dudes, dudes,
Dudes, dudes, dudes,
Are the Greensboro fair and radiant dudes.[21]

In addition to this excursion into parody Will also appended to the drama a burlesque of the type of Sunday

School literature then well known. Having in mind the Sunday School papers given to children in the primary departments, he wrote:

FOR THE INFANT CLASS

The Good Boy and the Poor Old Man

On a cold bad day a Poor Old Man, went down the road. He looked sad and wan. The chill wind blew his rags about. Ah, the Poor Old Man. Some boys from School did pass that way. The Bad Boys did say, Now we will Have some Fun. And so they threw stones and mud At him. What Cruel Boys! The Stones did Hurt the Poor Man. Some mud Did strike him in the Eye. And then the Boys did Shriek with Joy. John Ray had a Kind Heart. He felt sad be-cause he had thrown Some For-ty Stones, and had not Hit him once. John was a good Boy and went To Sun-day School. He said, Oh Boys do not Hurt the Poor Old Man, He is lame, and sad and Cold. The Old Man heard his kind words And a Tear stood in his Eye.

Oh Boys! said John—See—He is al-most Blind. Let us Take him down the Road, and push him in the River. Good E-nough the Boys did Shout. Then John Went up quite close and Said. Oh Sir do come with Us and we Will give you Food and you may Sit by a Warm Fire. The Poor Old Man could Not say A Word. He was So Cold. But he Reached Out and caught John Ray by the Scuff of his Neck. He then Wiped up the Pave-ment with Him and Broke his Collar Bone. Next he Slammed him a-gainst the Fence and Bust-ed his Spi-nal Col-umn, and Spoiled his Gen-e-ral Ap-pear-ance. Then he Tied him in A Knot and Jam-med him Through A Circus Bill-board. At first John Did Howl for all he was Worth, but he re-frained as Soon as the Vi-tal Spark had Fled. This sad Tale should warn All Boys not to Throw Mud and Stones In-dis-crim-i-nate-ly.

Some-times a Sad and Poor Old Man will turn out To be a
Bul-ly Boy with A Glass Eye.[22]

The following spring Will wrote a letter to Mrs. Hall,
which has remained unpublished until the present:

                              The Brush, La Salle Co. Tex. May 5/83
Dear Mrs. Hall,

I have been in a state of being about to write to you for a
mighty long time and hoping these few lines may find you the
same I submit to you the following letter which contains all
the news from this part of the world together with various
observations on general subjects. Everybody is well. Lee has
recovered & gone off on some trip—I don't know where. Dick
has gone to San Antonio to sell his wool.

I have just finished helping Dr. Wilson to move into his new
house, it is about 30 yards distant, consists of one room, he
will add another shortly. I expect you are so taken up with
weddings & marryings that you won't think as highly of this
letter as you ought to, but if you will read it over again in less
exciting times, its beauty and completeness will impress you
more. Won't you please in your next letter mention some more
about those ice cream & watermelon & 10th of May Celebra-
tions & Soda water & Presbytery & Concerts & picnics & dog
fights and other summer amusements. The more I hear about
such things the better I love this country & the more content I
am to stay here. Mab is progressing finely, can talk some &
understands everything you say to her, her hair is not at all
red, it is just the color of a dying fire coal, tenderly touched
by the flickering rays of the setting sun. The sudden change in
the size and style of my chirography is to be attributed to a
freak of my pen, which I am unable to rectify, and being a
thousand miles from any other, I shall have to ask you to
excuse it.

My sheep are doing exceedingly well thank you, the range is fine and they are in splendid condition but I haven't sheared any of them yet. They are all owned by other persons in the county.

I see that Capt. Geo. Gregory will deliver the memorial address in May & suppose that in consequence of which Jim Forbes will commit suicide. Give Dr. H. my best regards & wishes & tell him his friend Mr. Murchison sends his love & a kiss. Murch is at the Sany now with all his hounds, and he & Mr. Wm. Hall keep the wild cats & coyotes on the jump all the time.

Porter & Dalton seem to be getting proud, building stories & improving generally. Though I guess they will never again secure as accomplished & thoroughly scientific pharmaceutist as myself.

I see by the Bugle that Dr. Beall has returned from his bridal trip. I hope he will have good success hereafter, and lots of patients. Don't forget to write me, although this letter scarcely deserves an answer but I always look for a reply. A letter from you is of more value than many Bugles.

Very Truly Yrs.
W. S. Porter[23]

Often amused by the crudities of life in the ranch country, Porter liked to share his mood with those who could appreciate it. Since Mrs. Hall had seen the ranch, he furnished her with a description of Dick Hall's new house: "It has a tobacco-barn-like grandeur about it that always strikes a stranger with awe, and during a strong north wind the safest place about it is outside at the northern end." Continuing his report he said: "Cotulla has grown wonderfully since you left; thirty or forty new houses have gone up and thirty or forty barrels of whiskey gone down. The barkeeper is going to Europe on a tour next summer, and is thinking of buying Mexico for his little boy to play with."[24] No one has written a more accurate description of the "norther" so well known to all Texans:

There is a very pleasant little phase in the weather which is called a "norther" by the natives, which endears the country very much to the stranger who experiences it. You are riding along on a boiling day in September, dressed as airily as etiquette will allow, watching the fish trying to climb out of the pools of boiling water along the way and wondering how long it would take to walk home with a pocket compass and 75 cents in Mexican money, when a wind as cold as the icy hand of death swoops down on you from the north and the "norther" is upon you.

Where do you go? If you are far from home it depends entirely upon what kind of life you have led previous to this time as to where you go. Some people go straight to heaven while others experience a change of temperature by the transition. "Northers" are very useful in killing off the surplus population in some degree, while the remainder die naturally and peacefully in their boots.[25]

Further enumerating the happenings at the ranch, Porter wrote: "The chickens are doing mighty well, the garden produces magnificent prickly pears and grass; onions are worth two for five cents, and Mr. Hughes has shot a Mexican." The same letter revealed that "Ed Brockman has quit the store and I think is going to work for Lee among the cows. Wears a red sash and swears so fluently that he has been mistaken often for a member of the Texas Legislature."[26]

During the winter of the next year (1884) Porter wrote to Dr. W. P. Beall:

If you see anybody about to start to Texas to live, especially to this part, if you will take your scapyouler and sever the jugular vein, cut the brachipod artery and hamstring him, after he knows what you have done for him he will rise and call you blessed. This country is a silent but eloquent refutation of Bob Ingersoll's theory; a man here gets prematurely insane, melancholy and unreliable and finally dies of lead poisoning, in his boots, while in a good old land like Greensboro a man can die, as they do every day, with all the benefits of clergy.

A heretofore unprinted passage from this same letter reads:

Yes I wish I could come back to live in N. C. I know it's a better place than Texas to live in, but I've left it, and I'm not going to crawl back; if I come it must be in a coach and four so I guess I won't have the pleasure for sometime. I would like to see Ab Wilson & Dr. L[ogan]. I don't think it would be dangerous, for Dr. L. wouldn't try to catch me because his hair would get out of fix, and running would cause him to emit moisture through the pores,—he wouldn't sweat. While Ab I don't believe would get angry, although some people say he very often loses his patients.[27]

Will Porter's wish to return to Greensboro, but not in the same financial condition in which he had left, suggests his primary reason for going to Texas. Had it been health alone that he sought, he would have been more concerned about returning well than wealthy. If the spirit of adventure had actuated him, he would not have felt obliged to absent himself indefinitely. His correspondence reveals one torn between affection for his home place and the desire to succeed before returning. Another passage, hitherto unpublished, from the same letter reveals further his interest in Greensboro people:

I haven't heard anything from Ed Brockmann in a good many months. He went to San Antonio nearly a year ago, staid there a while, and then went farther west, I believe to Prisidio County, and I have heard no accounts of him since that time.

I am not surprised to hear of Messers. Michaux & Callum's developing into first class swells; I could see symptoms before my departure, and Bogart was the glass of fashion long ago. Has he acquired any more Cheek since I left? I used to think he had enough of his own, but he was trying to gather unto himself more.

Greensboro seemed remote from La Salle County, and the young man of twenty, looking eagerly for news of its society and pleasures, rode into Fort Ewell once a week for the mail. For one who could not feel himself at home amid the dangers and discomforts of Texas, the trip was a joy rather than a task, and Greensboro seemed to move a bit closer.

When he was returning to the ranch from one of his usual rides to the post office, the young mail carrier was forced by a violent thunder shower to seek refuge in the nearest shelter. Finding it already occupied by a band of ruffians, Will had no escape but was compelled to remain with them until the storm subsided. As the lightning flashed and the rain beat down, the members of the gang cursed and blasphemed. Their words and actions were horrifying to him; he was astounded and frightened. Arriving at the ranch greatly upset by the experience, he vigorously recounted the whole episode to Mrs. Hall.[28] Although such occurrences were not unusual, Will could not accept them as the cowboys did. Robbery and murder were sometimes committed by such gangs, and it was unsafe to travel without a gun. Now that he had experienced danger, the contemplation of it was not pleasant.

Moreover, Will continued to find that he was not cut out for ranch life. Much as he tried to adapt himself to it, he could not really learn to like it. The following March he wrote to Mrs. Hall in Greensboro:

I hope you will excuse this letter, not because I have a bad pen or am in a hurry, or because its the best I can do (I can write a much better letter), nor because its getting late, or suppertime, or anything else of that sort, but because its a product of La Salle County, which is sufficient excuse for a multitude of shortcomings.

Three years ago a man accused of having murdered 5 families and 263 children was tried not far from here, and the popular sentiment was that he should be severely punished, as the crime was proven beyond a shadow of doubt and the offence was too culpable to be passed over without notice in a law and order loving community, but the counsel for the defense proved by several witnesses that the prisoner had of his own free will and choice resided in La Salle county for a number of years. This of course convinced all persons that the poor man was really insane and he was at once released.[29]

This passage was deleted by Smith, as was the following one, which concluded a statement about returning to Greensboro only after financial success: "Then I will return; and I guess not before unless I can find sooner, a wealthy cattle man asleep with his ill gotten gains in his pockets and fall heir to his cash."[30] As no escape from the ranch offered itself, however, Will sought to make the most of his opportunities.

From the cowboys he learned to cook, which he was always to enjoy. He learned the cowboy songs, which he sang while strumming his guitar, and once in a while he invented stories for the entertainment of the others when evenings were long and still, and "It would not have been preposterous for one to tiptoe and essay to touch the stars, they hung so bright and imminent."[31] When a convivial mood seized him he accompanied the cowboys to Fort Ewell or to Cotulla, where they painted the town red. The entertainment was of the rough-and-tumble sort characteristic of the frontier, and in the lingo of the range, "They saw the elephant and heard the owl." More and more, however, Porter became the onlooker rather than the participant. He preferred not to have any set or regular tasks, but to take odd jobs not given to the steady workers. Will spent most of his time in the manner of Sam Galloway in "The Last of the Troubadours." He told funny stories, he sang songs, he smoked cigarettes and talked. "And he never sat up when he could lie down; and never stood when he could sit." Will like Sam spent most of his time lying on "a cool, canvas-covered cot in the shade of the hackberry trees." There he "rolled his brown paper cigarettes" and read whatever literature the sheep ranch afforded.

Having plenty of time on his hands, he revived his favorite practice of drawing caricatures of his associates. Rollins has recorded that with a piece of cardboard and pencil Will would amuse himself and entertain visitors by drawing caricatures and distorted landscapes to illustrate the day's happenings.[32] His reputation as a cartoonist began to spread beyond the boundaries of the ranch, and not long thereafter he was asked to become the illustrator of a book.

This book, never to be published, was called "Carbonate Days." The author, known as "Uncle Joe" Dixon, had been a mining prospector in Colorado, and it was a narrative of his personal experiences in the form of a novel. Dixon had never entertained any thoughts of writing, but his friend John Maddox of Austin finally convinced him that he could make more money writing a book than he could prospecting. As a result, he moved to the suburbs of Austin and started to work. One day Maddox came to him with news of a boy out on the Hall ranch who could "draw like blazes." Dixon went out to the ranch and decided to give the boy a chance. For three weeks he remained there while he and Porter made plans. During the daytime they discussed the story together, often while walking across the chaparral plains. Then at night Porter drew the pictures. They remained together constantly while the work was in progress, sleeping in a shack and spending the days roaming over the ranch.

When the pictures were finished there were forty of them in all, which Dixon pronounced "good and true to the life they depicted."[33] This was more than the author could say for his own efforts, however, for when Dixon returned to Austin and read his narrative through, he compensated for his lack of creative ability by a display of critical discernment and threw it into the Colorado River. When the astounded Maddox heard what had happened, he frantically organized a searching party to salvage the manuscript. After it had been fished out of the river, Maddox hastened all the way to New York, where to his great disappointment the soaked pages were pronounced too badly damaged to be repaired. In order to placate his friend, Dixon then wrote a burlesque, "An Arrested Movement in Southern Literature," telling of his brief career as an author and the loss to literature caused by the destruction of his work. Years later Porter wrote that he once drew the pictures for a book and when the author saw them he threw the whole thing into the Colorado River.[34]

While Will was illustrating Dixon's ill-fated book, Uncle Joe tried unsuccessfully to interest him in writing. Mrs. Hall had confided to Dixon that besides being able to draw, the boy had real narrative ability. When she added that he had told her stories which were as good as anything from the pen of Rider Haggard, Uncle Joe was impressed. Dixon and Porter had been assigned a rude little shack for their collaboration, and it was easy for the old prospector to retire there with Will and investigate the validity of Mrs. Hall's confidences. Uncle Joe soon agreed; moreover, he conceived a high respect for the boy's personality and urged young Porter to try his hand at writing for the magazines or at least at contributing to the newspapers. Will evinced no inclination for literature, however, and Uncle Joe finally gave it up as hopeless.

Apparently Will had no real idea of what he wanted to do. Riding to Fort Ewell for the mail seems to have been the only assignment he performed with regularity. Fort Ewell, J. Frank Dobie tells us in *A Vaquero of the Brush Country*, was made up principally of Mexicans and the storekeeper,[35] but about this time it suddenly developed a magnetic attraction for the young mail courier. A girl from Brenham had come out to visit her uncle, the storekeeper, and the little settlement took on a glow of romance. At first Miss Clarence Crozier rendered him speechless, for he was too shy to talk to her. Nevertheless, as he persisted in coming to the store, they finally became friends. To further his courtship, Will took to riding after the mail at unaccustomed hours, sometimes appearing at the combined store and post office just in time for supper. The ambitious aunt of the young lady did not approve of Will as a suitor. When her entreaties fell on deaf ears she resorted to bribery, in which she was successful, the promise of a white ostrich plume holding more allure than Will did in the eyes of

Clarence, who returned forthwith to Brenham and forgot the affair.[36] Young Porter's interest in her was likewise transitory, for although he might have become serious if she had remained in West Texas, he wrote back to Greensboro after her departure:

You are right, I have almost forgotten what a regular old, gum-chewing, ice-cream-destroying, opera ticket vortex, ivory-clawing girl looks like. Last summer a very fair specimen of this kind ranged over about Fort Ewell, and I used to ride over twice a week on mail days and chew the end of my riding whip while she "Stood on the Bridge" and "Gathered up Shells on the Sea Shore" and wore the "Golden Slippers." But she has vamoosed, and my ideas on the subject are growing dim.[37]

After Miss Crozier had returned home Will found life in La Salle County even duller than before he had known her. Now that he had tasted a bit of social activity, he began to long for all the pleasures enjoyed by young people in the towns; he wanted to go to dances and ice-cream suppers, to take his guitar and stroll forth to serenade. In short, he was growing restless on the ranch, and he wanted everything that he was missing. Despite his reserve and shyness Will Porter was of a gregarious nature, and it was the young man of the sheep-ranch days speaking for O. Henry in "The Hiding of Black Bill" when he said:

I've seen a lot of persons more entertaining as companions than those sheep were. I'd drive 'em to the corral and pen 'em every evening, and then cook my cornbread and mutton and coffee, and lie down in a tent the size of a tablecloth, and listen to the coyotes and whip-poor-wills singing around the camp.[38]

Although he did not know it, events were conspiring to end his career as a ranchman. The year 1885 was the last one in which the barons of the range were able to command a high price for their cattle. An era was ending, and Lee Hall, seeing what was coming, decided to dispose of his stock. During the spring of 1884, Dick Hall, in anticipation of his brother's actions, had bought land in Williamson County, where he shipped his flocks of sheep.[39]

Will found himself confronted with the alternative of going ever farther away from civilization or seeking his fortune in the city. Since a return to Greensboro was out of the question, he decided to try his luck in a Texas town. Life in the capital appeared attractive, spring was approaching, he had passed his twenty-first birthday, and he had never had any affection for sheep. Fortunately he received a welcome invitation from a Greensboro family in Austin, who agreed to Dick Hall's suggestion that Will might stay with them until he could find something to do.

Although he did not then realize it, his connections with the ranch were to prove of value to him later. When he wrote about the cowboys and the ways of the West he pictured them in a manner which could come only from first-hand observation. And when he wrote his stories in those later days, he forgot the inconveniences which had annoyed him, forgot how much he was bored by the life of the ranch, and how glad he was to leave it. In his maturity he pictured the cowboys and their customs in a manner that leaves no doubt of his admiration for them.

IV

The Austin Years

AUSTIN, when Will Porter arrived, was a town of only ten thousand people, but it was the capital of the state and in many ways a blend of the old culture of the South with the new. Will was welcomed there into the home of Joe Harrell, who had been born near Greensboro. The Halls, who always visited the Harrells on their trips to Austin, had only to remind Harrell who Will's people were to insure the young man's acceptance at once as a guest who was not permitted to pay for board or lodging. The Harrell household was like those he had known in his childhood, and there Will spent something like three years, living as one of the family, going and coming as he pleased, and sharing the pleasures of the Harrell boys—Harvey, Dave, Joe, and Clarence.[1] Occasionally he would leave the Harrells for a room downtown with two young men who had become his cronies, Will Anderson and Ed McLean. But these periods did not last long, and Will would return to the Harrell home, where a welcome always awaited him.

Those days in Austin were delightful for a young man just escaped from the sheep ranch before, as an O. Henry character said, ". . . the wool entered my soul."[2] With a determination that his associates should not be sheep, Will began prospecting for a job. When he heard that the Morley Drug Company needed a clerk, he lost no time in applying for the position. He was told that as soon as he could prove his qualifications, the place would be his, a stipulation which was easily and quickly met. Will's letter to Greensboro, asking for credentials, was answered on May 24, 1884, by a commendatory letter, signed by four Greensboro physicians, recommending him "both as a druggist and citizen" and by another letter, signed by the clerk of the Supreme Court and endorsed by the register of deeds and the postmaster, praising him as a "young man of good character, an A No. 1 druggist and a very popular young man among his many friends."[3]

Will went to work with an enthusiasm which quickly began to cool. After the relative freedom of the ranch, the long and regular hours in the drugstore were confining. One of his reasons for leaving Greensboro had been his desire to escape from the drug counter, and the longer he worked and the more he thought about it, the less he liked it. Within two months he gave up the job with the explanation that drawing soda had proved too much for him.[4]

It was some six or seven months before he again obtained employment. Finding himself with nothing to do except lounge around the Harrell home, he would drop into the cigar store owned by Joe Harrell and help out by waiting on customers or working on the books. So long as there were pleasant diversions and no urgent necessities, he was quite content to let things rock along. This was his natural unaggressive temperament, which did not diminish his popularity. Gifted with a keen wit and graced with pleasant manners, he entertained his friends with his ready humor and his ability to sing and play the guitar. While waiting like Mr. Micawber for something to turn up, Will continued to make friends at dances and bazaars or on serenading parties. Almost everybody who knew Will Porter in Austin declared him thoroughly likable.

Among his best friends was John Maddox, an important real estate executive whom Porter had met in connection with the book-illustrating episode of the ranch days. Finding that Will was without a job, he offered him a position with the real estate firm of Maddox Brothers and Anderson. The offer was accepted, and Porter began work in the fall of 1885, under the supervision of Anderson.[5] Employers like Maddox and Anderson were pleasant to work for, and the latter, who was the father of one of Porter's best friends, treated the young man like one of his family, taking him into his home, where Will and his son became even closer associates. Under Anderson's tutelage Porter developed into an accurate bookkeeper, worked diligently, and liked both his work and his employers. With a salary of one hundred dollars a month Will was so contented with the position that he remained with the firm until January 1887 when he left to enter the Texas Land Office.

Very soon after coming to Austin, Porter had become a member of the Hill City Quartet, which was well known throughout the town; the other members were Howard Long, R. H. Edmondson, and C. E. Hillyer. Long was a handsome young man whom the local merchants often furnished with clothes as advertising for their merchandise; later he became a professional model for men's clothing. Edmondson was a sober and religious young man, who never failed to kneel in prayer before retiring, no matter who was present. Hillyer, the fourth member, became a well-known businessman of Belton, Texas, where he was a deacon in the Baptist Church.[6] Although there were other serenading groups in Austin, the Hill City Quartet, largely because of Porter's membership, soon became so popular that they were invited to sing in three different churches. It was not, however, for their church work that memories of the group outlived its membership. Serenading was their real object, and to this they devoted their talents handsomely. Will wrote to Dave Harrell, then visiting on his ranch:

Our serenading party has developed new and alarming modes of torture for our helpless and sleeping victims. Last Thursday night we loaded up a small organ on a hack and with our usual instruments made an assault upon the quiet air of midnight that made the atmosphere turn pale.[7]

Amateur theatricals were another form of popular entertainment to which Porter was attracted, for he always had a fondness for the stage and for theatrical people. He appeared as Sampson in the performance of *The*

Black Mantles at Millet's Opera House on January 26, 1886,[8] the cast also including his friends Long, Hillyer, and Edmondson. Will later claimed that it took him two years to live this down, but that he finally succeeded. This was the only time, so he recalled, that he was not in the chorus, although he remembered being in *Pinafore, The Bohemian Girl, The Mikado,* and *The Chimes.* "Down in Texas at one time," he stated, "I belonged to a first rate musical association (amateur)."[9] Will confided to Mabel Wagnalls that this company was so successful that they played in other places than Austin. The minstrel show with its jokes, songs, and dances further engaged his talents and remained something he always enjoyed. He professed to be bored by classical compositions, but was delighted with music of a lighter vein, the lively wit and sprightly music of Gilbert and Sullivan attracting him, as did the popular tunes of the day.

Like other Texas cities Austin had its militia company, the Austin Grays, in which Will Porter became a lieutenant.[10] He also became a National Guardsman, joining the Texas Rifles, in which he rose to the unspectacular rank of corporal.[11] A number of people later prominent in Texas were members of the Texas Rifles, but the majority of them were more interested in having a good time than they were in military science and tactics. The parades and encampments offered opportunity for fun, and even when the company found itself called to duty, the members regarded military service more as a holiday than a serious task.

During a strike the Texas Rifles went to Fort Worth to guard a depot from damage by the strikers, an assignment which all the guardsmen regarded as a pleasure trip since military discipline was never strictly enforced. Porter, who at the time was attracted by a girl who was visiting in Waco, wired her to meet him. As the train pulled into the "Katy" station at Waco on its way to Fort Worth, Porter was seated proudly on the cow-catcher, from which he waved his greetings.[12]

An encampment was held at Lampassas which afforded further opportunity for amusement. While attending one of the dances at a near-by hotel, Porter and some of his friends who had overstayed their leave learned that a corporal's guard was approaching to arrest them. There was no chance to escape, but Porter explained their plight to the other dancers, who agreed to help them. One young man met the squad at the hotel door with the plea that the guardsmen stack rifles outside to avoid frightening the ladies. The obliging corporal complied and, stacking their rifles, he and his men entered the front of the hotel just as Porter and his friends were slipping from the back of the ballroom. Hastening around the building, the fugitives silently seized the rifles of the unsuspecting squad who were searching inside, and headed back for camp. To get past the sentry at the entrance a ruse was cleverly enacted: some of the men carried the rifles stolen from the guards, while the rest pretended to be in custody. Porter, acting as corporal, called out sharply, "Squad under arrest," and they passed safely into camp.[13] Porter enjoyed his membership in the Austin Grays; he relished dressing in his uniform and parading through the streets to be gazed upon, especially by the young ladies, for whom he waxed his mustache and wore his uniform whenever the occasion permitted.

About this time he renewed his friendship with the Cave family, whom he had met upon his arrival in Texas, and became a frequent caller at their home. Through them he was introduced to many pleasures, and with Lollie Cave he enjoyed a whirl of parties and gaiety. She frequently invited him to dinner and later recalled: "Bill was very fond of corn pone. His tastes were simple and good food to him meant turnip greens, ham gravy, mashed potatoes, fried chicken, hot biscuits, 'lasses pie, and chocolate cake."[14] She remembered him as a continual perpetrator of pranks. Once during a dance he appeared unexpectedly dressed in her grandmother's Mother Hubbard and carrying her pet dog, Pom, dressed as his partner. Will and Lollie were together often, and Will eventually proposed; but although Lollie admired him, she did not think them suited to each other and refused his offer of marriage. Yet they remained good friends.[15]

On one of their outings she recalled that Will Porter used the name "O. Henry," apparently for the first time, applying it not to himself but to a stray cat which he nicknamed "Henry the Proud." The cat would come to him when he called, "Oh, Henry," or "O. Henry," but when he called simply "Henry" the cat would not answer.

Will began to identify himself with the name, and one day he said to the cat that they should both be christened. Then, much to the disgust of the cat, he proceeded with the ceremony. Afterwards he wrote a composition signed "O. Henry," of which Lollie remembered: "We called it 'A Soliloquy by the Cat.' This was in the summer of 1886, and it was the first time William Sidney Porter ever signed the name of O. Henry."[16] There is also a picture reproduced from her autograph album with the inscription, "O. Henry—Polly O" and the date "1886." No earlier use of the name has been discovered.

Porter was not impressed with his own literary efforts in this first venture signed "O. Henry." It was, however, an amusing composition in which he used every conceivable word having the syllable "cat" in it. He was not inclined to write anything more, as his thoughts at the moment were concerned with securing a good position. Dick Hall had been elected State Land Commissioner of Texas in 1886. When Porter appealed to him for a place in the Land Office, he was assured that an appointment would be granted provided he could prepare himself within a period of three months. He set to work at once, and when three months had elapsed he entered the Land Office as assistant compiling draftsman. Porter served here from January 12, 1887, to January 21, 1891, at a salary of one hundred dollars per month.[17] As this was the same salary which he is supposed to have received in his former position, he probably anticipated promotions which did not materialize. Nevertheless those four years spent in the Texas Land Office were happy ones, perhaps the happiest of his entire life.

A natural draftsman, he did not find the work difficult. Furthermore the situation provided him with interesting material to study. He was able to observe at first hand the struggle between the settlers and the land sharks who tried to swindle them out of their holdings by legal manipulations. As most of the records in the office were in a state of confusion, the proper papers to settle a dispute were so often lacking that the Commissioner was forced to rely on his own judgment to reach a decision. These cases of disputed land fired Porter's imagination with their dramatic possibilities. The old office building itself appealed to his emotions and in later years he turned to it as inspiration for plot and setting. Rollins has noted that one story was so frankly based on Commissioner Hall's methods that after O. Henry's real name became known the author forbade its publication in book form.[18] The story "Georgia's Ruling" was later published in *Whirligigs* after O. Henry's death. Another story growing out of his experiences in the Land Office was "Witches' Loaves." The draftsmen always used stale bread to erase pencil marks from their drawings, and O. Henry later recalled an incident of a clerk's ruining a drawing by picking up a piece of buttered bread by mistake. Changing his story to that of a sentimental shopkeeper who suspected a prominent architect of being a starving artist because he bought stale bread from her, he achieved a surprise ending by introducing his recollection of the draftsman's mistake. "Bexar Script No. 2692" owed its conception to the old building in Austin, not only for its setting but also for its plot. "Buried Treasure" was based on the experiences of a group from the Land Office who went hunting for hidden gold in Pease Park.[19]

While working in the Land Office, Porter was tempted to pick up a few extra dollars in real estate speculation. Buying a small piece of stray property in Wilbarger County for fifty dollars, he kept it for a few months and sold it for nine hundred.[20] This was apparently his first and last excursion into the realm of speculation. Although he did attempt to help a family back in Greensboro to settle claims to an estate, he seems to have made no further effort to augment his own fortunes. When he was not busy with his work as draftsman, he was far more interested in drawing than in seeking profit through speculation. A number of old maps are on file in the Land Office, decorated with cartoons or pictures of animals native to the county. Along the borders of these maps Porter drew flourishing scrolls, filling in the spaces with buffalo, trappers, frontiersmen, wagon trains, and mythical goddesses, in keeping with the location of the county. He further satisfied his desire to draw by making sketches on the walls of the old building to amuse his fellow workers.

Since he could not draw cartoons as much as he liked while at work, he drew them for his friends when paying social calls. The young ladies especially liked to have him draw in their albums. Shortly after his entry into the Harrell home he had drawn "Father Harrell" carving a turkey. It is reported that the Harrells offered to send him to New York to study art and that later Charles Anderson made the same offer, but Porter was not interested.[21] As long as he amused people by his drawing he asked nothing more of it.

When the cornerstone of the state capitol was laid, the Austin Grays took part in the ceremony and celebrated that night by giving a german. At this dance Will Porter first met Athol Estes.[22] She was the most popular young lady of the evening and they were attracted to each other at once, for they had everything in common. Both had been born in the Old South, both were of generous natures, kind, and gentle. Moreover, both liked to sing, enjoyed books together, and as each possessed a keen sense of humor, their pleasures were shared equally. Athol had been born in Clarksville, Tennessee, in 1868.[23] During this time Negro uprisings were frequent around the town, and to escape this danger her family moved to Nashville. Not long after Athol's birth her father died, and when she was six years old her mother married again. This second husband, G. P. Roach, who had lived in Pittsburgh before coming to Nashville, had two daughters, both several years older than Athol. Shortly before the marriage Roach had become involved in financial difficulties which resulted in the loss of almost everything he owned. Consequently he offered to release Mrs. Estes from her promise, but she refused, saying they

would start all over again together. They were married
and moved to Austin, where they placed Athol in school.
During the school session of 1886-87 Athol began to talk
to her school friends about Will Porter.

The description of Della in "The Gift of the Magi" is
derived from O. Henry's memories of Athol. Small and
slender, she possessed many of Della's characteristics.
"She had a habit of saying little silent prayers about the
simplest everyday things." Frances G. Maltby tells us,
"Athol was a belle from babyhood to maturity by sheer
right of charm."[24] She was always animated and happy.
Her complexion was described by a former schoolmate
as "peach-bloom pink and white."[25] Light brown hair
curled beneath the blue bonnet she frequently wore
matching her blue eyes. Dressed in her ruffled dimity,
she was charming.

At night Will and a friend would call on Athol, and
they would all sit together on the porch steps and sing.
The Roach home was a popular spot, and Porter was not
the only one who liked to visit it in the evenings, for
Athol had numerous suitors. When the weather was good,
especially in the spring and summer, Will and Athol
liked to drive along the near-by roads, arched with bor-
dering trees. They often went to entertainments together
and found that their tastes were always congenial. It
was at one of these, a drill by the young ladies with
Porter as instructor, that Athol became engaged to him.[26]
While his courting was in progress Will drew a number
of cartoons for Athol and sometimes wrote amusing little

notes to her, notes she would show to her interested schoolmates. When still in grammar school Athol, who was an exceptionally good student, had received the Peabody Medal for the best record in English composition. As she appreciated good writing, she delighted in books. This pleased Porter, who was equally gratified by her enjoyment of the pictures he drew for her.

Although Athol's parents had no objections to Will Porter as a person, they did object to his uncertain financial condition; they would have preferred to have Athol marry some suitor with more promise of worldly success. Mrs. Roach in particular had a marked preference for a rival named Zimplemann. Athol, however, had confidence in Will and gave him her word in spite of her family's opposition. Despite Athol's promise Will was not satisfied, and he continued to feel uncertain about the outcome of his suit. He knew how Mrs. Roach felt, and the knowledge made him uneasy. Consequently he made up his mind to elope.

One day in July 1887 the opportunity presented itself. Mrs. Roach asked her daughter to run an errand for her, and Athol, who was wearing a torn dress at the time, did not even bother to change it. Remarking that she would be home again before she would be likely to see anyone, she hurried away. Athol had no idea of marrying Will Porter on that day, and their meeting was purely by chance. Porter took advantage of his opportunity. Without giving her a chance to demur, he insisted that they should be married immediately. Athol tried to reason

with him, but he refused to listen. Before she had time to
realize what was happening, she found herself on the way
to her wedding. Somehow Will managed to get a license,
and then with the friendly aid of Charles E. Anderson,
they went to their pastor, the Reverend R. K. Smoot.
Alighting from the carriage, Athol, who had not even
been given time to change her apparel, complained that
her dress was torn. Will stooped to pin it carefully for
her and then they walked into the house. With Mr. and
Mrs. Anderson for witnesses, the ceremony was performed in the front parlor. Athol and Will were married
Friday, July 1, 1887. The hour was not midnight, as
has been claimed, but nine-thirty in the evening, and the
carriage was not borrowed, but a "lit hack" which had
been rented from one Miller, a liveryman.[27]

As soon as the ceremony was over, the couple went to
the Anderson home where Will had been staying. Anderson offered to serve as an ambassador for reconciliation
with Athol's parents and left to break the news. The
Roaches forgave the young couple at once, and there was
never again any mention of their former opposition.
They had never harbored any real objection to Will
Porter, and since Athol had married him, they wished
them nothing but success and happiness. Indeed, in later
years both Mr. and Mrs. Roach were Will Porter's
staunchest friends, standing by him faithfully in his distress.

In "Sisters of the Golden Circle" O. Henry wished for
time to turn backward and give him once again even a

small bit of his honeymoon. "Just an hour, dear fairy, so we can remember how the grass and poplar trees looked, and the bow of those bonnet strings tied beneath her chin—even if it was the hat pins that did the work."[28] For him "bride" remained the "word of words in the epiphany of life and love."

Will and Athol stayed at the Anderson home for six months. Then, according to Edmunds Travis, they lived in a house on East Fourth Street, and later moved to a little cottage on East Eleventh Street, only a few blocks from the Land Office where Will was employed.[29] Although their funds were small, they took delight in acquiring what furniture they could afford. Their home was their chief interest, and they exhibited with pride the new bedroom suite, equipped with two mirrors and purchased on the installment plan.[30]

The married life of the Porters started off happily. They were admirably suited for each other. Will's pride in Athol and his love for her stimulated him to greater efforts, while Athol, despite the fact that she was never strong and was frequently ill, proved a devoted wife. For one thing, she encouraged him to write. Porter, always reticent, depreciated his own ability, and Athol's appreciation of his work was the encouragement he needed. Athol felt sure that he could earn extra money by his pen, and her faith was justified. They had been married only a few months when Will received his first payment for a contribution to *Truth*, a check for six dollars. Two sketches, "The Final Triumph" and "A Slight

Inaccuracy," were accepted by this magazine. It did not matter so much what he was paid: what was important was that he had actually sold something. On September 4, 1887, the *Detroit Free Press* wrote to him, requesting that he send them something each week. With this encouragement, backed by Athol's belief in his ability, he continued his efforts. Soon Porter was also contributing to *Up-to-Date*. The real literary career was in the future, however, and this was but the prologue.[31] A promise of what was to come, these early writings finally led to his first full-length short story, which was accepted by the S. S. McClure Company on December 2, 1897.[32] Entitled "The Miracle of Lava Canyon," it testifies that Will Porter wrote successfully for publication before he left Austin.

For a time, life in Austin was pleasant. Athol was near her mother, she had numerous friends, and the Texas capital was never dull. There were frequent dances and germans, parties and amateur theatricals. There were church socials, which played an important part in the lives of the Austin citizens. Will and Athol sang in the choir of the Southern Presbyterian Church, and likewise belonged to a musical organization which gave frequent entertainments. When the weather was good, as it usually is in Austin, they took long drives together. Will liked to get out of doors, Athol shared this inclination, and together they sought the open country, sometimes carrying a book along to read in a quiet spot. At times Will would go fishing, but it was not so much catching fish which he sought as it was the excuse to get away from town. Will never learned to care for hunting, and when he was prevailed upon to go on a trip, he left most of the shooting to the others. What he liked best of all was the companionship around the campfire, when stories were told and songs were sung.[33]

Yet the happiness of Will and Athol was not to continue uninterrupted. The first sorrow of the young couple was the death of their child, a boy who was to have been named after his father.[34] Borrowing Roach's phaeton, Will and Athol would drive out to the cemetery and put flowers on the grave. Their grief was deep and these visits were frequent, but they were too young to remain downcast, and as time passed they regained their happy manner of living. Their happiness was increased by the birth of a daughter, whom they christened Margaret Worth, born September 30, 1889.[35] Unfortunately, with the birth of Margaret, Athol became dangerously ill, and for weeks it was feared that she would not live. After she started to recover, she was still so ill that any idea of the Porters' maintaining a home was out of the question. Will closed their home, and carrying Athol in his arms, placed her in the phaeton and took her to her parents.

They remained with the Roaches until the following summer. As Athol had improved greatly and Margaret was now big enough to travel, Will arranged a journey. During the summer of 1890, Athol and Margaret accompanied Mrs. Roach to Nashville, going from there to

Greensboro, where they visited Aunt Lina.[36] It was decided that Athol and Margaret should remain in Greensboro until October, when they were joined by Will. He
enjoyed displaying his attractive wife, who was again in
good health, and Margaret, who was a pretty and healthy
child. When they left to return to Texas, they received
a promise from Aunt Lina to visit them. According to
Mrs. Anna Boyers, a cousin of Athol, Porter and his wife
went to Greensboro again in 1891, returning to Texas by
way of Nashville.[37] There they visited Athol's relatives,
and Will saw something of the city he later described
so well in "A Municipal Report." This trip, which was
their last, was probably financed in part by Mr. Roach;
Will could scarcely have been able to pay all the expenses of a journey which came within a year of the
previous one.

In Austin they began housekeeping all over again.
Will liked to prepare certain foods and particularly enjoyed taking pains to broil a steak. Often when friends
dropped in for dinner he insisted upon cooking the meal,
always serving one of his favorite dishes, onions cut
into cubes and soaked in vinegar. If a reluctant guest
sought to refuse, he would urge that it was both palatable
and pungent.[38] These dinners with Will as chef were a
source of great pleasure.

During the visit to Greensboro in 1890, Porter became
interested in the claims of a Greensboro family to a large
estate in Texas, and urged them to attempt to regain their
title to it. He was in a position in the Land Office to know

the inside of land deals in Texas, and after his return to Austin he wrote two letters back to Greensboro, seeking power of attorney for himself and Ed McLean.[39] Since this power of attorney was never sent we do not know what success Will would have had in a legal matter so foreign to him.

The old account books of the Land Office reveal that he usually drew the greater part of his salary in advance. To augment his income—he was earning only a few dollars here and there from the contributions he sent to the journals—he turned to the occupation of illustrating a book. Some of the sketches with which Will had amused his associates came to the attention of Thaddeus A. Thomson, who arranged for Porter to draw the illustrations for a book then being written by J. W. Wilbarger. The narrative, *Indian Depredations in Texas,* was to be published in Austin by the Henry Hutchings Printing House. The pictures ran to twenty-six, and woodcuts were made of them by T. J. Owen, a local engraver. Porter seized upon the most vivid moments in the narrative, producing illustrations of such episodes as "Scalping of Josiah Wilbarger" and "A Comanche Warrior Dragging to Death Mrs. Plummer's Child." Another illustration, executed with a blending of the humorous and the grotesque, involved an escapade with a skunk, which Will reproduced with realism.[40]

The Porters finally settled in a little cottage on East Fourth Street, where they lived longest while in Austin. In a large barn which stood in the back yard, Will fitted up a crude study. By the time he left Austin he had collected there a library of about a thousand volumes, all of which were later destroyed by fire.[41] In this study he wrote the humorous articles he hoped to sell, or tried his hand at sketchy pieces of journalism. Some of these pieces were done to please Margaret, who was an audience to be entertained with both stories and drawings. Not only did he amuse Margaret; he became a great favorite with all the children in the neighborhood, inventing new games for them, telling them stories, and drawing funny pictures. Some of these pictures still exist, and they have lost none of their freshness. The valentines he drew for Margaret are especially charming. One was of Uncle Remus, Br'er Rabbit, and the Little Boy;[42] another was a picture of a neighbor to which he had pasted cotton to represent hair and whiskers. He enclosed a description of the valentine:

The Sad Story of Mr. Raats

Mister Raats was a little old man with cottony hair and a reddish nose. He had a tiny little boy named Arthur. But they called him Tom because it wasn't his name.

Mister Raats made Tom work every day while he himself only smoked his pipe and read the newspapers.

Tom worked so hard that he grew so fast that he became so much larger than his father that one day Mrs. Raats got a pair of Tom's old trousers and cut them down to fit Mr. Raats.

The picture shows Tom's glee and the sad face of Mr. Raats who seems to feel keenly his sad fate.

Let all parents take warning and not make their children work when they should be playing.[43]

In 1890, Commissioner Hall was an unsuccessful candidate for governor, losing the election to James Stephen Hogg. As a result Porter felt compelled to resign his position, and left on January 21, 1891, to accept another in the First National Bank of Austin as teller and part-time bookkeeper.[44] It was a sad mistake, for Will Porter was never intended to be a banker. Moreover, the work in this bank was of a particularly complicated nature and it was made more difficult by the manner in which business was conducted. The officials in the bank, indeed, seemed to have no rules at all. Overdrafts on accounts were allowed continually, and an officer of the bank might not even bother to write a check,[45] merely saying to a teller that he was drawing out some money. Sometimes he even forgot to mention the matter to the teller until a day or so later. Porter soon realized that he had made a mistake in accepting this place, yet he had no alternative but to stay on until another means of earning a living presented itself. To escape from his job and add to his always insufficient income, he turned his attention once more in the direction of journalism.

During two of the summers in which Porter worked at the bank, he and his family occupied the home of the Halls while they were away on their ranch.[46] A lovely old brick house surrounded by cedars, it was situated across the Colorado River opposite Barton's Spring, and stood on a hill affording a fine view of the town. It was fortunate that Margaret could have such a place to play all summer, and her parents watched her with pleasure.

As soon as his work in the bank was finished, Will hurried home to his family, and at night he and Athol strolled about the lawn, singing their favorite songs, or went to one of the many informal parties to which they were invited.

Late in the summer of 1893, almost everyone in Austin who could manage it was planning to visit the Chicago World's Fair. Athol's parents were going, and they offered to take care of Margaret on their return so that Athol might make the trip with some friends. At first Athol planned to go, but when the time arrived she refused to leave Will alone to work; since Will had given her the money for the trip, she preferred to spend it on something he could enjoy too. Consequently, when Mrs. Roach returned from the fair and called upon her daughter, she found the Porter house decorated with new curtains, new mattings on the floors, and two new wicker rockers. Athol had bought the furnishings without Will's knowledge and worked all morning to have everything ready as a surprise for him.[47] It was well that his wife could be so happy with so little. Although Will Porter spent some twelve years in Austin, at no time could he really have been termed successful financially. His income was never much more than a hundred dollars a month, and it was not always that. He was never able to buy a house. But finally when an opportunity which might lead to financial improvement came from an unexpected source, Will seized it.

W. C. Brann, editor of the *Iconoclast*, had decided to

leave Austin and offered to sell his plant for $250. To Porter it looked as if the chance he had been waiting for had come. Here was escape from the drudgery of the bank; with a publication of his own, his talent would be turned to a practical purpose. Talking the matter over with two friends of his Land Office days, Herman Pressler and Will Booth, Porter persuaded them to sign his note, and the sale was made. Will Porter became a newspaperman in March 1894.[48] Two issues of the paper were printed under the *Iconoclast* masthead, but when Brann requested that he be allowed to retain the use of the name, Porter relinquished it and rechristened his paper *The Rolling Stone*, which made its first appearance on April 28, 1894, with a subtitle announcing that it was "Out for the Moss" and that the price of subscription was a dollar and fifty cents payable in advance.[49] The edition for May 12, 1894, announced that S. W. Teagarden had been made manager, but these first issues of the paper were almost wholly the production of Porter, who was assisted by Athol and Roach. From time to time during the one brief year of its existence *The Rolling Stone* acquired new managers and new circulation directors.[50] The course of the paper was not smooth, despite a promising start with two issues of one thousand copies, each selling rapidly. This early success caused Porter to print six thousand copies for the third edition which he distributed free, hoping to sell advertising space to the businessmen of Austin.

The size and format of the paper were changed more

than once during its existence, and new features were introduced from time to time. Addresses announced in the publication testify that it also changed its location frequently. At first it was an eight-page weekly, but toward the end of its career *The Rolling Stone* began to bounce and skipped a few issues. The make-up was mostly cartoons, humorous sketches, bogus news accounts of the country weekly variety, and anecdotes. All the drawings and most of the writing were done at first by Porter himself, but after a few issues his friends began to contribute. As the circulation increased, syndicated articles by Bill Nye were added. Scattered within the pages of the paper are typical examples of O. Henry humor, as a few culled at random will demonstrate:

A high lonesome—a diamond solitaire.

A bare living—a ballet dancer.

Effectual calling—calling a minister to a church that pays $10,000.00.

A married couple may travel very well in double harness, but they are often separated by a waggin' tongue.

A poor man may be a gentleman, but it is mighty hard work.

One of the most popular features of the paper was the section called the "Plunkville Patriot." It was always set in type which had first been intentionally confused so that the advertisements and personals were garbled in the fashion of a small-town weekly. By no means an invention of Porter's, the idea had been used by Mark Twain in 1889 in *A Connecticut Yankee,* and had a long history before that. Begun on October 27, 1894, just a month before Porter resigned from the bank to give his entire attention to the paper, the "Plunkville Patriot" lasted until the final issue.[51] The supposed editor of this burlesque publication, Colonel Aristotle Jordan, composed items for that page of *The Rolling Stone* which are still amusing. When Colonel Jordan failed to receive the postmastership of Plunkville, the "Patriot" carried a scathing denunciation of the national administration. When Adams and Company, grocers, discontinued their $2.25 advertisement, the "Patriot" took revenge in this fashion: "No less than three children have been poisoned by eating their canned vegetables, and J. O. Adams, the senior member of the firm, was run out of Kansas City for adulterating codfish balls. It pays to advertise." On another occasion the Colonel, wishing to protect his fellowman, hastened to announce to those bent upon a kindred pleasure that "There is a dangerous hole in the front steps of the Elite Saloon," and in novel fashion he made the following announcement of his candidacy for mayor:

Our worthy mayor, Colonel Henry Stutty, died this morning after an illness of about five minutes, brought on by carrying a bouquet to Mrs. Eli Watts just as Eli got in from a fishing trip. Ten minutes later we had dodgers out announcing our candidacy for the office. We have lived in Plunkville going on five

years and have never been elected anything yet. We under-
stand the mayor business thoroughly and if elected some people
will wish wolves had stolen them from their cradles.[52]

The Colonel is a true O. Henry creation, and through
this fictitious character Porter was able to give outlet
to his buoyancy and to write as humorously as he desired.

When Porter felt certain that *The Rolling Stone* would
pay him enough to live on, he quit the bank and devoted
his entire attention to it. After work on the paper was
finished at night, Porter and Dixie Daniels, his managing
editor, roamed about the town, wandering up side streets
and alleys in search of the unusual. Sometimes they went
into the tougher sections of the town on excursions which
Porter called "bumming." Wandering about, they encountered specimens of all kinds of humanity, ranging
from the hopeless down-and-outers to more prosperous
citizens in a whiskey-soaked condition. Porter thoroughly
enjoyed these night rambles, for he was developing into
a sympathetic and accurate observer. Moreover they
served in the nature of adventure, which he always
needed. A natural romantic, he became seriously interested in treasure hunting. Even to this day legends sur-
vive of vast fortunes buried in the Southwest, and many
have spent their lives in vain search for them. Stories
of the early Conquistadors who buried their gold when
attacked by Indians, tales of Mexican paymasters forced
to abandon the money they were carrying to Santa Anna's
army, accounts of outlaws like Billy the Kid who buried
their loot to escape being captured with it—whatever the

source, the formula was the same. These legends fascinated Will Porter; he became enthusiastic over the
prospects and went to work with all the energy of the
old-time treasure hunter.

Vic Daniels has recounted how he, Dixie Daniels, and
Porter went on a treasure hunt in 1895.[53] There had been
persistent rumors of a buried treasure supposed to have
been taken from a murdered paymaster of the Mexican
army. An intricate narrative revealed how the murderers
quarreled and then killed one another, and how the
treasure had been buried by the last of the assassins.
Porter and his two friends discovered a map and several
charts in the possession of an aged Mexican who claimed
to be a descendant of the man who had buried the treasure. He sold them the papers with the understanding
that he should be properly remembered when the treasure
was unearthed. The three men began poring over the
map and charts and then carefully examined the vicinity
of the outlined territory. When the tree markings indi-
cated on the map were located, the exact spot of the loot
was finally determined. So sure were the three treasure
hunters of having located the reputed twenty thousand
gold pieces that they began to make plans for spending
the money. These included not only furnishing *The
Rolling Stone* with the capital it needed so badly but
also purchasing another paper to be consolidated with it.

On an appropriately dark night the three set out,
armed with tools for digging, a Colt pistol for protection,
and a bottle of whiskey for inspiration. Arriving at the

spot, they began to dig, interrupting their labors with
frequent pulls at the bottle. Just as the hole had reached
a depth of seven feet and the contents of the bottle had
been drained, the searchers were electrified by a horrible
screeching and howling. Whatever was shrieking was also
dancing around the treasure spot in a circle. Out went
the light and with it all thoughts of treasure. There was
a wild scramble to get out of the hole and back to the
buggy. With no concern save putting distance between
themselves and this terrible noise, they rushed for the
buggy. Off they went as fast as their horse would carry
them, bumping into trees and bushes, and stopping only
once to untangle the horse. The next day, they learned
to their chagrin the origin of their fright. The noise had
been caused by an escaped lunatic from a near-by
asylum, who had seen their light and joyfully made for
it. So crestfallen were Porter and his confederates that
they concealed their secret from the puzzled authorities,
who concluded that the lunatic must have dug the hole
himself, for they regarded the presence of a Colt pistol
as proof of his intentions to dig in and fight to the last.
In his haste to leave when the shrieking commenced, Vic
Daniels had become confused in the dark, and mistaking
the empty bottle for the pistol had armed himself there-
with and carried it home. This episode ended Porter's
treasure hunting.

In January 1895, an Englishman, H. Ryder-Taylor,
came to Austin from San Antonio and convinced Porter
that he could make *The Rolling Stone* a national success,

if given a partnership in the venture. Having failed to make a profit in Austin, Porter had already visited San Antonio the previous December to see what could be done toward working up a circulation in that city. *The Rolling Stone* for January 26, 1895, announced that it was to be "published simultaneously in Austin and San Antonio, every Saturday,"[54] with Ryder-Taylor as manager of the San Antonio edition. The only good which came from this alliance with Ryder-Taylor was that it caused Porter to spend some of his time in San Antonio, then as now the most interesting city in the Southwest. Unfortunately for the prospects of the paper, however, he allowed Ryder-Taylor to talk him into entering a political fight then under way in San Antonio, a bad blunder as it alienated most of his readers there. This ended whatever hope he may have entertained of continuing the paper in both cities, and it eventually led to the end of *The Rolling Stone*. It had been steadily losing subscribers and advertisers in Austin because of a cartoon which had angered the German residents, and since the paper had never attained an average circulation of more than fifteen hundred copies, the losses suffered in both cities could not be regained. On April 27, 1895, the last issue of *The Rolling Stone* came from the press, and Porter was forced to close his plant.[55]

After *The Rolling Stone* had ceased, Porter spent several months seeking another connection, and in July 1895 had decided to accept a job in Washington, D. C., when Athol became ill. Such a long trip was out of the question, and Will refused to go without her.[56] As no other positions became available closer by, there was nothing to do but try to earn a living as a free-lance writer. He sold a few items here and there to papers throughout the country, and by October 1895 he was writing chiefly for the *Cleveland Plain-Dealer*.[57] The trials that beset a free-lance writer and the experiences that he underwent have been good-naturedly fictionized by O. Henry in "Confessions of a Humorist."

Friends of Porter in the meantime had been active in his behalf. Ed McLean had sent a copy of *The Rolling Stone* to R. M. Johnston, who controlled the *Houston Post*. After reading through this number of the paper, Johnston arranged for an interview with Porter, which concluded in his being added to the staff. The work was at first general, but any employment that was steady would have been acceptable by this time, particularly when it was of a journalistic nature. Now Porter moved Athol and Margaret to Houston, where his first column appeared in the *Post* on October 18, 1895.[58] At first his writing was captioned "Tales of the Town," which was soon changed to "Some Postscripts and Pencillings," and finally became "Some Postscripts." Although he started with the paper under the real name of Sidney Porter, he always referred to himself in his column as "The Post Man." As he had done in Austin, he searched the town for his materials. Going to the old Hutchins House, he would sometimes sit for hours in the lobby, studying the

faces of the guests. Another favorite spot for observing
humanity was the Grand Central depot, where many a
drama in miniature was enacted before his eyes.[59] Always he sought the places where he could study character
and meet people from all walks of life.

His assignments were largely in the nature of chores
at first, like reporting society items, which he asked
Athol to do for him, but they gradually became more interesting, and his salary increased from fifteen to twenty-
five dollars a week. When Johnston discovered Porter's
ability to draw, he gave him the further duty of supplying the paper with cartoons. The *Post* was in the midst
of a particularly hot political campaign and badly in
need of Porter's talent. The cartoons he drew about the
political situation attracted much attention at the time
and were widely copied by other papers.[60]

Continuing his work for the *Post* as a literary Jack-
of-all-trades, Porter drew cartoons and comic sketches
akin to the modern comic strip, some of them to illustrate
his own compositions. He did not devote his writing entirely to his column, which appeared at irregular intervals, but preferred to create lengthy sketches, extrava-
ganzas, poems, topical commentaries, and humorous
quips. These excerpts from life, like those written for
The Rolling Stone, were not short stories; they were
amusing anecdotes, suggestive of what was to come, but
showing no qualities of literary mastery in themselves.
They were what the *Post* wanted, however, and Porter

did well in his work. Appreciated by his employer and liked by his associates, he seemed to be well settled in the position of newspaper writer.

While Porter was working on the *Post* he renewed an old acquaintanceship with Mrs. Lollie Cave Wilson, then living on a farm located near the city. The Porters gladly accepted her invitations and on their visits the farm became to Margaret a playground and an exciting new world. Once they experienced a thrilling ride when the horse ran away with the buggy and nearly turned them over. Another time Will gratified his old inclination for playing pranks by feeding whiskey to Mrs. Wilson's pet rooster.[61] Apparently he was resuming his old ways of life in Houston, where he and his family were beginning to feel at home. Successful in his occupation, he might have stayed there if events had not brought an abrupt end to his plans. On February 10, 1896, an indictment was filed in Austin charging:

That on the 1st day of November, A. D. 1894, the said W. S. Porter being then and there Teller of the 1st Natl. Bank of Austin, did embezzle and convert to his own use the sum of $4,702.94 with the specific intent to injure and defraud the said 1st Natl. Bank of Austin.[62]

This indictment was returned unexecuted on the next day by Marshal Ware with a notation that Porter was no longer in the district. A warrant was then issued to the Marshal of the Eastern District, who ordered his deputy to execute it. Will Porter was placed under arrest in Houston on February 14, 1896, by J. S. Williams, who turned him over to Marshal Ware. As soon as Porter's friends in Houston heard what had happened they acted immediately to help him. Johnston wired Ed McLean in Austin: "Porter arrested; meet him at train and make bond for him." When the train arrived in Austin, McLean was there, ready to help. Contrary to his usual nature, Will Porter got off the train "sullen and noncommittal." All that McLean could get out of him at that time was a terse "I made a mistake of five hundred dollars in paying out money."[63] Assuring him that "everything would be all right," McLean at once made arrangements for Porter to return to Houston, which he did.

Although he resumed his work on the *Post,* his column came out at uneven intervals, appearing, according to Mary S. Harrell, only four times in February, seven in April, and three in June.[64] As the court records reveal that February was the month of his indictment and arrest, and he was again in Austin in March, while at home Athol's health was growing continually worse, he was unable to bring out his work with any regularity. Johnston was entirely sympathetic, paying Porter his full salary and even giving him money.

Porter again appeared in Austin before the clerk of the court on March 16, 1896, to declare in a signed statement that he could not prepare a proper defense without examining the books of the bank covering a period of four or five years. Since this would take considerable time he asked for continuance of the case. Although he had been arrested February 14, 1896, he declared that he had been unable to procure counsel to conduct his defense until March 14. The statement continues:

The defendant further states that he resides in the City of Houston, where he has lived for about four months; that for the past thirty days his wife has been ill, a greater part of the time, being confined to her bed; that being a comparative stranger in said city, defendant's presence at his wife's bedside was absolutely required, she having no friends or acquaintances in said city to give her necessary attention, and that she is now in that condition. That for the reasons stated, it has been beyond the power of defendant to visit the City of Austin and spend sufficient time to make any personal examination of the books in said bank.[65]

Afterward Porter returned to Houston, where he continued to write for the *Post*, the last column appearing June 22, 1896. When Porter started back to Austin in July to stand trial—his friends had successfully stopped one indictment but failed to stop the second—the editor of the *Post* and another friend gave him $260 toward his expenses.[66] The story of how he arrived at Hempstead, and there took the train for New Orleans instead of continuing to Austin, has been often told. In view of all the facts, it seems highly probable that his action had been planned in advance, although the opinion has been generally accepted that he suddenly decided to flee while waiting for a train. Porter may have been advised to go away for three years and seek dismissal under the statute of limitations, for he was provided with more money than he needed for a trip to Austin.

Rollins records that the staff of the *Post* assumed that

Porter had gone to Cuba, for the night editor wrote on
July 10, 1896:

The reporters who went to see the Austin train off saw Mr.
Porter there, and he has never been seen since. Our presump-
tion naturally is that he took the east bound Southern Pacific,
which leaves [Houston] about the same time. . . . We know
he speaks Spanish fluently and think that a man who is a
fugitive from justice might naturally try to bury himself in
Cuba.[67]

Early one rainy morning after Will Porter's departure
from Houston, Mrs. Richard Hall, whose home was then
in that city, was awakened by a Negro boy calling her
husband. When Hall arose to question the boy, he learned
that a lady and a child wanted to see him. The lady was
Athol and the child was Margaret. The Halls received
them and made them comfortable, and as soon as possible
made arrangements to send them to Athol's parents in
Austin, who had no idea of her plight.[68] In this fashion
the life of Will Porter and Athol Estes in Houston was
brought to a close. They were never again to have a home
of their own, for when Will returned to Texas he found
Athol ill beyond recovery, and he himself forced to stand
the trial from which he had fled.

❦ V ❧

New Orleans and the Tropics

How long Porter stayed in New Orleans is still a mystery, but he could not have remained there more than a brief period. He did, however, become familiar enough with the town to write convincingly about it. His first story published under the name of O. Henry, "Whistling Dick's Christmas Stocking," had its setting in Louisiana. One of his best stories, "The Renaissance at Charleroi," pictures New Orleans and an old plantation near-by. Some of the finest passages in all his writings concern the old French quarter, like this one from "Blind Man's Holiday," in which something of its spirit seems actually to linger:

The Rue Chartres, in New Orleans, is a street of ghosts. It lies in the quarter where the Frenchman, in his prime, set up his translated pride and glory; where, also the arrogant don had swaggered, and dreamed of gold and grants and ladies' gloves. Every flagstone has its grooves worn by footsteps going royally to the wooing and the fighting. Every house has a princely heartbreak; each doorway its untold tale of gallant promise and slow decay.[1]

82

Little is known about Will Porter's life in New Orleans. We learn from Mrs. Wilson that upon reaching the city he assumed the name of Shirley Worth. His first letter to Athol, sent to her through Mrs. Wilson, stated that he had a room near the famous restaurant of Begué, where the rich and distinguished ate breakfast at eleven o'clock in the morning.[2] He must have enjoyed the strangeness of the city, and from his stories we may draw suggestions of what he did there. In later life he often referred to it, giving the impression that he left Texas because he was dissatisfied and went to New Orleans to take up literary work in earnest.

He was not long in finding something to do. Going to work as a newspaper reporter, he quickly became intimate with a group of newspapermen who had rented an old rookery down in the French quarter and employed one of the best Creole cooks in the city. Here Porter lived for a time, and less fortunate reporters considered it a rare treat to receive an invitation, because of both the company and food.[3] Near-by was a popular barroom, the Tobacco Plant Saloon, where the barkeeper was particularly clever at picking up scraps of useful information. Newspapermen from all the different papers stopped in the saloon regularly to see if he had any tips, and the place became something of a newspaper club. Porter was a frequent visitor, often drinking more than was good for him, but he was well liked by his fellow reporters, who saw in him nothing out of the ordinary.[4]

For a while he was on the payroll of the *New Orleans*

Delta, later changing for brief periods to other papers, one of which was the *Picayune.* What he enjoyed writing most was the human interest story, but he was not very successful in selling these efforts. The newspapers at that time were more interested in straight news accounts than in feature articles, a circumstance which forced him to turn to reporting.[5] Not very adept in gathering the news himself, he was far better at writing it, showing more skill in characterization and motivation than he did in a statement of facts.

However, he saw much of the old city; in "Phoebe" he describes drinking cognac in the little red-tiled café near Congo Square. "Cherchez la Femme" takes the reader to a "Creole-haunted café": "It is small and dark, with six little polished tables, at which you may sit and drink the best coffee in New Orleans, and concoctions of absinthe equal to Sazerac's best."[6] Especially favored customers were invited into a small back room where they reclined in armchairs by a big window, peaceful and contented. "From the little courtyard a tiny fountain sent in an insinuating sound of trickling waters, to which a banana plant by the window kept time with its tremulous leaves."[7] Porter also wandered down St. Charles, Chartres, and Royal streets, where the old dealers in china and silverware and furniture had their shops, and there he gathered impressions which he later used in his stories.

Yet he was not destined to continue as a newspaper reporter for long; his stay in New Orleans was drawing to a close. Being a fugitive from justice, he had to seek refuge in a place safe from apprehension; and since New Orleans was not such a place, he decided to join the colony of missing men in Honduras, where there was no extradition. There were three or four banana companies using small chartered vessels to trade along the coast of Honduras, and it was as a passenger on one of these steamers that he came to Trujillo.[8]

The only account of Porter's life in Honduras comes from Al Jennings, a train robber who, with his brother Frank, was also a fugitive from justice. When Jennings arrived at Trujillo, he saw an American flag over a small bungalow, which turned out to be the American consulate. Porter was sitting on the veranda, clad in white ducks and looking as though he owned the establishment; in fact, Jennings at first mistook him for the consul. Porter apparently made friends with him at once, and Jennings claimed that they traversed practically the entire coast of South America together. Many of the stories recounted in *Cabbages and Kings* took place directly under Jennings' observation; some of them, it is claimed, were part of his own escapades. The stories may seem theatrical and exciting, but life in Honduras was strange and sometimes turbulent. One of the incidents was a Fourth of July celebration which Porter later made into a story. During the celebration, according to Jennings' account, they had been drinking freely; feeling the effects of the liquor and hearing a noise in the street, they dashed out of the cantina, staging something of a riot on their own account. Yelling at the top of their lungs and firing six-shooters, they put the native military force to rout. When the fracas was over, they were surprised to learn that they had taken part in a revolution. This episode involved them in political difficulties which eventually forced them to leave Honduras,[9] but meanwhile Will enjoyed the romantic beauty of this small tropical country, and met many of the people whom he later transferred to the pages of his first book. Here he made the acquaintance of "Beelzebub" Blythe, Henry Horsecollar, Frank Goodwin, Clancy, John DeGraffenreid Atwood, and all that host of fantastic creations he was later to incorporate into his stories. He did no writing in Honduras, but afterward, when he composed his romantic narratives of this exotic country, he drew vividly upon his recollections. Trujillo became Coralio, which

. . . reclined, in the mid-day heat, like some vacuous beauty lounging in a guarded harem. The town lay at the sea's edge on a strip of alluvial coast. It was set like a little pearl in an emerald band. Behind it, and seeming almost to topple, imminent, above it, rose the sea-following range of the Cordilleras. In front the sea was spread, a smiling jailer, but even more incorruptible than the frowning mountains.[10]

At one time Porter confided to Jennings that he never intended to return to the States and was looking for a place to anchor safely. When he had found one and had located a suitable school for Margaret, he intended to send for his family. In the meantime he wrote regular letters back home, sometimes sending them to Louis Kreisle, who then delivered them to Athol. At other times

the letters were sent to Mrs. Wilson in Houston, who remained anonymous, readdressing and relaying them to
Edd R. Smith in Austin, who handed them to Athol.[11]
The letters which Athol wrote to Porter in return were
sent first to Houston, then to New Orleans, and from
there to Honduras. In his letters, too, Porter expressed
his desire to establish a home in the tropics, and disclosed
that he did not spend all his time in the ease and con-
viviality pictured by Jennings. He wrote once that he had
been digging ditches to earn a livelihood. Likewise he
revealed there were times when he was without a place
to stay or anything to eat save what he could forage.[12]
Mrs. Wilson has said that she herself received three letters from Porter while he was in Central America, one
from Honduras, one from Puerto Cortes, and one from
Trujillo.[13]

Meanwhile Athol, in spite of her poor health and her
parents' willingness to provide for her, wanted to earn
something until Will could once again take care of her
and Margaret. She started a course in business college
but was unable to finish because her health failed under
the strain. Persisting in her efforts, she made a point-lace
handkerchief, which she sold for twenty-five dollars, and
then, like Della in "The Gift of the Magi," spent the
money for her husband's Christmas box. A month later,
when Porter learned from Mrs. Roach that Athol, with a
temperature of 105 degrees, had packed this box for him,
he knew that she was dying. Abandoning all thought of a
home in Honduras, he started back to Austin. He knew

that if he returned there he would have to stand trial, but he had only one thought: to reach Athol before she died.[14]

Passing through New Orleans, he telegraphed to G. P. Roach on January 21, 1897, "Wire me twenty-five dollars without identification quick. Can't get my check cashed. W. A. Bright."[15] The money was sent by Roach the next day, and the distressed husband hurried on to Athol. Arriving in Austin unobserved, Porter hastened to the Roach home, where his wife and daughter awaited him. And only then, determined to face the consequences, he made known his presence in Austin. The trial records reveal that he appeared in person in court on the first day of February 1897.[16]

The Trial

AFTER appearing in court and satisfying the authorities
that he would not again attempt to escape, Porter was
allowed to make a new bond. Dated February 12, 1897,
this bond took the place of the original one given by him
for four thousand dollars, with G. P. Roach and Herman
Pressler for security. The forfeiture of his old bond, declared upon his disappearance, was now set aside and his
bondsmen were not made to pay.[1] Herman Pressler told
C. Alphonso Smith that the court did not collect on the
bond but simply doubled it.[2] With his bond secure Porter
was not brought to trial for another year; the authorities
made no attempt to press the case.

Athol did not have long to live; she was too weak even
to walk. Porter did everything in his power to make her
last days happy. He would carry her to and from the
buggy, in which they took long drives along the roads
of their sweetheart days. On Sunday mornings Will
drove under the windows of the Presbyterian church,
where they could hear the services and listen to music
they had sung together; then, just as the congregation
was beginning to depart, Will would quietly drive away.
All during Athol's illness her stepfather paid her doctor's

bills and aided Porter in every possible way. Just a little more than five months after Will returned, Athol died, on July 25, 1897.[3] She was buried quietly, and her funeral expenses were paid by Roach. Will and little Margaret, remaining apart from the others, attended the funeral in a carriage to themselves. Margaret, sobbing continually, could be quieted only by her father, who placed her in the buggy as he had done her mother, and drove out into the country, where she finally went to sleep. The second night after Athol's death was a repetition of the first; again Will had to place Margaret in the buggy and drive out into the open before he could quiet her.[4]

People in Austin, especially Mr. Roach, sympathized with Will Porter and showed their friendship by coming to his aid. This generous old gentleman had aided Porter before by investing a thousand dollars in *The Rolling Stone*, and now he continued to stand by him. All in all, according to Smith, he gave his son-in-law a sum of about ten thousand dollars. On October 23, 1915, he affirmed his belief that Porter, had he lived, would have repaid every cent. He impressed Smith as "a fine fibred old gentleman not embittered."[5] Mrs. Roach, who always contended that Will was innocent of any wrongdoing, supported him loyally. Others came to his assistance, including his old friend Mrs. R. M. Hall, who wrote the prosecuting attorney, asking him to be merciful.[6]

In considering Porter's trial, it is necessary to examine the events leading up to it. In 1895, before Porter moved to Houston, the first grand jury that had looked into the matter returned a "No Bill."[7] They were influenced largely by the testimony of Frank Hamilton, a friend of Porter's and part owner of the bank, who made such a sincere and impassioned plea in his behalf that they decided not to indict. The bank examiner thereupon complained that influential friends of Porter were seeking to bring pressure to bear in the case. Having secured evidence which he thought should result in a conviction, he reported the district attorney, R. U. Culberson, for neglect of duty.[8] Edward I. Johnston, who had failed in his efforts to secure an indictment, was replaced by F. B. Gray, who was determined not to let the matter drop. Culberson's attitude had reflected the feelings of Porter's associates, both in and outside the bank. He had been informed that the bank owners, who had themselves made up the shortages in 1894, were anxious to let the whole affair be forgotten. No depositor had lost anything, the bankers were satisfied, and Porter's friends were asking that the prosecution be stopped. But when F. B. Gray managed to secure an indictment based on evidence which he felt strong enough for a conviction, Culberson had no choice.[9]

The term of court itself was opened February 7, 1898, with Judge Thomas S. Maxey presiding, and on February 15 Porter was taken into custody by the United States marshal, who committed him to the Travis County jail. Two new indictments were filed against him on that date. Hyder E. Rollins has recorded the dismissal or consolidation of the original indictments with these new ones.[10] Porter was arraigned on three indictments, one of which had been filed against him on February 10, 1896, and the other two on February 15, 1898. The first indictment (No. 1148) charged that Porter, while acting as teller of the First National Bank of Austin, had embezzled $299.60 on November 12, 1895. One of the later indictments (No. 1174) charged the embezzlement of $554.48 on October 10, 1894; and the other (No. 1175) declared Porter to be guilty of embezzling $299.60 on November 12, 1894. No. 1175 was corrective of No. 1148 as it referred to the same charge.[11] Porter was accused of only two misappropriations, which were the two counts on which he was convicted.

When Will Porter found himself faced with the two charges of embezzlement, his attorneys, Ward and James, filed the usual demurrers that the indictment in each case was not sufficient in law. Moreover, they filed a motion to quash the indictment, listing seven reasons for their action, which were, in brief: (1) The indictment failed to charge any offense against the laws of the United States. (2) The indictment failed to describe the bank sufficiently. (3) It did not charge Porter with converting the funds to his own use or of having any fraudulent intent. (4) The indictment was indefinite, uncertain, and insufficient. (5) It did not inform the defendant of how the embezzled funds may have come into his hands, or in what capacity he may have held them. (6) It did not allege that the funds came lawfully into the possession of the defendant by virtue of his employment at the bank. (7) Finally, the indictment did not set forth whether the property taken was money or funds.[12]

When this motion to quash the indictment was overruled by the court, Porter's attorneys brought up the statute of limitations, stating that prosecution was thereby barred. The defendant also claimed that "the Government has offered no testimony to show that this defendant has ever at any time been a fugitive from justice."[13] When this motion, as was to be expected, was overruled by the court, Porter and his attorneys countered with a motion to dismiss the indictment, giving the two following reasons: (1) As the District Attorney had admitted that Indictments No. 1148 and No. 1175 both constituted the same charge, "This defendant is therefore now being required to answer at the same time two distinct and separate indictments found by different grand juries for the same identical charge." (2) The government had offered no proof of the embezzlement of legal tender money. This motion to dismiss the indictment was likewise overruled.[14] On the same day Porter's attorneys came forward with a number of special charges.[15] They insisted the offense charged in each case was barred by the statute of limitations and that no proof was offered that the defendant had ever been a fugitive from justice. When these special charges were ruled not applicable by the court, the defendant's lawyers objected to the court's definition of a fugitive from justice.

Nearly all the actual evidence presented in the case

was lost by fire—even the stenographic notes taken at the time of the trial were later destroyed—but the fragmentary scraps remaining, together with the review of the case made in New Orleans by the Federal Court, present a clear picture of what happened:

A collection and credit slip from the First National Bank of Waco was sent to the Austin bank under the date November 10, 1894, for the amount of $299.60. On November 12, a credit slip for this amount was made out and sent to the Waco bank. Two months later, on January 16, 1895, J. K. Rose of the Waco bank wrote to the bank in Austin, saying, "You do not credit $299.60." He noted at the same time, "There is a further difference in our account of $100.00," and asked for an early report on the statement of his bank. To this, R. J. Brackenridge, president of the Austin bank, wrote in reply on January 17, 1895, saying that a recheck had shown an error in the balance of the Waco bank which was being corrected. The error, which had occurred in November or December of 1894, was apparently the $299.60 mentioned by Rose.[16]

This $299.60 was the amount embraced by charges No. 1148 and No. 1175. At the trial, witnesses testified that both the credit slip which had been sent to the Waco bank on November 12, 1894, and the letter which accompanied it were in Porter's handwriting. Witnesses further stated that the usual procedure would have been to make the proper entry in the books on the following day; however, from the evidence given in court it appeared that the entry was not made until some time later. The jury were convinced from the evidence presented that Porter had accepted the draft, sent a credit slip to the Waco bank, and then failed to enter the amount in the books. As the amount was still not credited when Rose wrote his letter to Brackenridge, it is evident that the entry was made later.[17]

The other count upon which Porter was convicted, charge No. 1174, accused him of embezzling $554.48 on October 10, 1894. On October 8, 1894, E. L. Gwartney purchased a draft for the sum of $554.48 on the San Antonio National Bank. Gwartney testified that he paid for the draft in cash at the time he bought it. Gwartney further testified that "to the best of his belief and recollection" he had always bought his drafts from Porter. It was further brought out that Porter was absent from his place at the bank only during noon, and Gwartney, who was with the Singer Sewing Machine Company, never bought any drafts at that hour. A bookkeeper in the San Antonio bank, R. L. Herff, testified that this particular draft had been paid by the San Antonio National Bank on October 10, 1894. The bookkeeper in the Austin bank, John H. Whites, who made the entries from the stubs of the detached drafts, could find no entry for the draft in question, although the stubs supposedly contained complete information. Another draft was drawn on the same day and still another was drawn apparently after hours, but the draft for $554.48 was not posted, and nobody could find any entry crediting the San Antonio bank with that amount. From this testimony the jury concluded that Porter had accepted the cash for the draft and then failed to enter it.[18]

Porter's attorneys exhausted every legal means to secure an acquittal: they insisted that the charges were barred under the statute of limitations; they declared that their client had never been a fugitive from justice; they again pointed out that two of the indictments referred to the same transaction. However, as nothing in Will Porter's life is better established than the fact of his flight, the point they hoped most to establish failed completely. Moreover, Judge Maxey's ruling that the second count was merely a correction of the first stopped their efforts in that direction.[19] Seeking a technicality of any sort, they charged again that no proof had been given that the funds taken were legal tender. Then, having failed on all technical points, the lawyers finally put forth the good character of the defendant in a plea for his release.

With the evidence in mind and having considered the special charges of Porter's attorneys, the jury were ready on February 17, 1898, to hear Judge Maxey's instructions to them, "to determine whether the defendant embezzled the two amounts mentioned, or either one of them, and to render your verdict accordingly."[20] After pointing out that the defendant, if found guilty of embezzlement, was liable to imprisonment of five to ten years, Judge Maxey then defined the word "embezzlement" in its technical meaning:

There must be actual and lawful possession or custody of the property of another, by virtue of some trust, duty, agency or employment, committed to the party charged; and while so lawfully in the possession and custody of such property, the person must unlawfully and wrongfully convert the same to his own use, in order to commit the crime of embezzlement.[21]

He made it clear to the jury that embezzlement was not necessarily theft. Even though there had been no actual loss to anyone, even though the money had been replaced by Porter or by his friends, the charge remained. Porter was not charged with "stealing" or with causing anyone to "suffer a loss," but with taking money entrusted to his care and using it. However, he reminded them that the law presumes a person to be innocent until he is definitely proved guilty, saying: "If, therefore, upon a full consideration of all the facts and circumstances in evidence, you entertain a reasonable doubt of his guilt, you should give him the benefit of it and acquit him."[22] He further suggested that the jury consider the evidence offered as to the defendant's honesty, uprightness, and integrity prior to his indictment, and that wherever the testimony appeared doubtful, the character of the accused should be given due consideration.[23]

The jury on the same day returned the following verdict: "We, the Jury, find the defendant guilty as charged in the indictments numbered 1148, 1174, and 1175 respectively."[24] Judge Maxey pronounced that he be imprisoned in the Ohio State Penitentiary at Columbus for a period of five years. The sentence was the lightest that

Porter could be given under the law, and to make things as easy as possible for him, it was temporarily suspended.[25]

Porter's attorneys promptly filed a motion for a new trial, which was overruled by the court on March 25, 1898, Judge Maxey stating that when W. S. Porter had been asked on February 17 if he knew of any reason why sentence should not be pronounced against him, "He answered nothing in bar thereof." Porter's attorneys then made the move of filing two bills of exception to the sentence, both of which were allowed by Judge Maxey. They were filed on March 31 after term time of the court and in vacation by agreement of District Attorney Culberson, who continued to give Porter fair and sympathetic treatment.[26] The attorneys followed this with a petition for a writ of error, which was promptly granted by Judge Maxey. Accordingly a bond of $250 was posted by Porter with Roach and Ashby S. James as sureties, and an appeal was made to the United States Circuit Court of Appeals at New Orleans which was sealed and allowed on April 20, 1898, by Judge Maxey.[27] Porter, as the endorsement of Marshal Siebrecht shows, was committed to the prison in Ohio on April 25, 1898.[28] The judgment of the District Court of Austin was affirmed by the Circuit Court of Appeals at New Orleans on the following December 13, 1898.[29]

Opinion in Austin after the trial was divided. There were those who claimed that the bank examiners, being disgusted with the lax manner in which the bank was run, decided to punish someone as an example, and Porter became the scapegoat. Another theory held that Porter was shielding somebody. But the rumor has persisted that he put the money into *The Rolling Stone*. Luther W. Courtney has summarized it thus:

One of the last circulation managers for *The Rolling Stone* told me in 1935 that he had made a careful study of the matter of Porter's trial. His study showed that Porter's income from salary, sale of papers, and advertisements during the period of publication was insufficient to run the paper after deduction of Porter's living expenses. It further showed that the insufficiency was almost the same amount of money for which Porter was indicted for embezzlement.[30]

Porter certainly needed money, probably for *The Rolling Stone*, and in his position of teller he was able to divert funds to his own use. Those who knew him at the time did not believe that he actually intended to defraud anyone or that he was guilty of any criminal purpose. His case was similar to one in his own story of a Texas banker, "Friends in San Rosario," in which a technical infraction of the law was committed, but not a moral one. The tragedy that it constituted in his own life and Athol's was out of proportion to the importance of the original lapse.

ᴄ VII ᴘ

Prison Interlude

Wʜᴇɴ Porter entered the penitentiary at Columbus in the spring of 1898, he lost his identity to the world. He did not know, of course, that his five-year sentence would be shortened for good behavior, and he could not foresee that within three years and three months he would emerge as O. Henry, the short-story writer known with delight to his readers and sought after by publishers. He looked upon the future without hope, and only the existence of Margaret made life seem worth living.

The relationship between Margaret and her father had always been particularly close. She had shared his worry over her mother's health, and after Athol's death she naturally came to signify to him many things that her mother had meant. She gave him the only incentive for not succumbing to his disaster; it was partly for her that he began to write. In the letters he sent her from prison we see plainly his concern for her happiness and his desire to hide his disgrace from her. He wrote again and again to tell her how tired he was getting of staying away from home, promising that when he returned he would never leave her. Always he admonished her to be happy and have the most enjoyable time she could. "Now, Margaret," he wrote only a few weeks after he entered prison, "don't you worry about me, for I'm well and fat as a pig."[1] Never a word did he breathe to her of his despair and misery.

Sending her presents whenever he could get the money to buy them, he waited with anxiety for the news of each story which he mailed, for upon its success depended his ability to buy her such things as the newest Uncle Remus book. "I send you twenty nickels to spend for anything you want,"[2] he wrote to her, and in another letter he said, "I have been expecting to have something to send you, but it hasn't come yet, and I thought I would write anyhow."[3] To satisfy her queries as to why she did not have her father with her as the other children did, he told her that he was too busy writing for the magazines and newspapers all over the country to have time to come home. So well did he succeed in guarding his secret that Margaret did not suspect that anything was wrong. He proudly and lovingly complimented her: "I think you write the prettiest hand of any little girl (or big one, either) I ever knew."[4] He wrote to her about her birthday and about Christmas, longingly saying, "I wish I could come home and light up the candles on the Christmas tree like we used to."[5]

Always anxious because of the delicate constitution which he was afraid his daughter might inherit, he reminded her, "When I come home I want to find you big and strong enough to pull me all about town on a sled when we have a snow storm."[6] Wishing to encourage her in her studies, he advised what he must have discovered from his own experience: "When one grows up, a thing they never regret is that they went to school long enough to learn all they could. It makes everything easier for them, and if they like books and study they can always content and amuse themselves that way even if other people are cross and tiresome, and the world doesn't go to suit them."[7]

Margaret was being cared for by her grandparents. The dates of Porter's letters to her reveal that she and "Munny," as she called Mrs. Roach, left Austin and moved to Tennessee sometime between July 8 and August 16, 1898, shortly after Porter's imprisonment. They went to the home of Mrs. J. A. Boyers, a relative in Colesburg, about forty miles from Nashville, where for nine months Margaret found out what country life was like. At this time the child thought that her father was working in a drugstore in Columbus. Roach paid all of Margaret's expenses during her stay at Colesburg, and continued to do so after he took her to Pittsburgh, where Margaret attended grammar school.[8] We know from Porter's letters to her that her grandparents had taken her to Pittsburgh before May 17, 1900.

Whether Porter could have endured his imprisonment without having Margaret on the outside is doubtful. His sense of shame was touched deeply, and he suffered to the limit of his endurance. The physician of the penitentiary said that in all his experience of handling over ten thousand inmates he never knew a man who was so humiliated by his experience. In a letter to Mrs. Roach, written shortly after entering the prison, Will told her there was absolutely not one thing in his life either at the present or in prospect that could make it of value: "It will be better for everyone else and a thousand times better for me to end the trouble instead of dragging it out longer."[9] The prison itself must have been a place of terror and misery. Al Jennings, who was serving a sentence there at the same time, has pictured its cruelty in his book *Through the Shadows with O. Henry,* which one might suspect exaggerated the horrors of the place, except that Porter himself has these revealing sentences in his correspondence which corroborate Jennings' accusations: "Suicides are as common as picnics here." "Consumption here is more common than bad colds at home." "I never imagined human life was held as cheap as it is here." "The men are regarded as animals without soul or feeling."[10] But terrible as it was at the time, it is doubtful if we should have had O. Henry, the short-story writer, if Will Porter had not gone to prison.

With the time to write, and the desire to do so in order to earn money, he began in earnest. Tradition has it that Porter sent the stories to New Orleans, where the sister of a New Orleans banker who was in the prison with Porter mailed them to the magazines. When his first story signed "O. Henry" appeared in *McClure's* in 1899, under the title "Whistling Dick's Christmas Stocking," a major figure in the history of the American short story had entered upon his profession. There are twelve stories which

Smith claims were written in prison, although Porter may have written more.[11] It was there that O. Henry met the original of Jimmy Valentine, the handsome thief of "A Retrieved Reformation," who took hearts as well as money, and the characters in many of the later stories of confidence men suggest the penitentiary as their source. At any rate, before his sentence was up, people were reading his stories and wondering who O. Henry might be. Of course, all that could be learned of him was rumor, and Will Porter, in changing himself into O. Henry, took special care to see that nothing but vague rumors were circulated. We do not know how much O. Henry made from these first stories, except that he was paid forty-five dollars for "Georgia's Ruling." Of this money, he told Mrs. Roach that he was going to send twenty-five dollars to John Maddox, to whom he must have been in debt.[12]

The stories he is known to have written while in prison deal chiefly with adventure in settings in the Southwest, the Southern mountains, and Central America, regions strange to the usual magazine readers. Absorbed in writing them, he occasionally forgot his surroundings, and his resentment, at first so strong, finally gave way to resignation which was not without hope. "I often get as blue as anyone can get," he said, "and I feel as thoroughly miserable as it is possible to feel, but I consider that my future efforts belong to others and I have no right to give way to my own troubles and feelings."[13] There is

a definite attempt to be more cheerful in O. Henry's sub-
sequent letters to Mrs. Roach. He told her that he was
treated with consideration by the prison officials, that his
room was large, airy, and clean, and that he was allowed
to walk about a big well-kept yard, filled with flowers and
trees. As night druggist in the prison hospital, he was
really much better off than the average prisoner. He was
allowed to sleep on a cot in the hospital rather than in a
cell, and he no longer had to eat with the others. His
record shows a model prisoner, so willing, obedient, and
faithful that he was released on a shortened sentence for
good behavior on July 24, 1901.[14]

When he left Columbus, O. Henry went to Pittsburgh,
where Margaret was living with her grandparents, remained there until the spring of 1902, and continued to
work on his short stories. Not quite sure that he wanted
to keep the name of O. Henry, he signed some of them
Sydney Porter, and occasionally he used such names as
Olivier Henry or S. H. Peters. It was not until he went
to New York that he became O. Henry once and for all.

The man responsible for bringing him to New York
was Gilman Hall, associate editor of *Ainslee's* and
later associate editor of *Everybody's Magazine*. He had
written to O. Henry about his stories before the latter left
prison, and he now wrote to him in Pittsburgh, urging
him to come to New York. Evidently O. Henry replied
that he needed money to make the trip, for Hall, who

eventually became a close friend, sent one hundred dollars.[15] Then he sent another hundred. Nothing happened, the time was long past when the unknown author was due, and Hall was beginning to despair. Finally, when he had given up, feeling that he would never succeed in getting this elusive writer to New York, O. Henry appeared.

✑ VIII ✑

New York and Success

IN THE spring of 1902, O. Henry had his first glimpse of his "Little Old Bagdad on the Subway." As Smith has truly said, "If ever in American literature the place and the man met, they met when O. Henry strolled for the first time along the streets of New York."[1] The beginning of his eight years there, however, was not auspicious. He spent a night or two in one of the cheap hotels along the water front and then set out to meet Richard Duffy and Gilman Hall, the editors who were responsible for bringing him to New York. From the moment of their first greeting they liked the new writer so much that the relationship between O. Henry and Duffy and Hall, especially Hall, soon became one of friendship rather than business. On that first afternoon, letting editorial matters wait, they took their visitor out for a stroll, pointed out landmarks which would assist him in finding his way about, and gave helpful answers to his many questions about life in New York. It was not long before he located himself in a little French hotel on Twenty-fourth Street between Broadway and Sixth Avenue.[2]

O. Henry lost no time in getting to work. He had come to New York to write and almost immediately he began

107

to turn out a number of first-rate stories. Consequently he did not have long to wait before magazine editors began to seek him out and request material. When his story "Tobin's Palm" reached the office of *McClure's Magazine*, it came into the hands of Witter Bynner, who greeted it with enthusiasm. When the head manuscript reader rejected the story and returned it to the author, Bynner insisted so strongly that it was the best manuscript he had ever seen in the office that McClure asked to read it. The delighted Bynner then went in search of the author and the manuscript, with the result that "Tobin's Palm" appeared in *McClure's* and a friendship ensued between the young poet and the short-story writer.[3] Working hard, O. Henry continued to produce with regularity stories that met with favor, both from the editors and the public.

The high point of his production came after he had been in New York for more than a year and a half. When the *New York World* signed a contract with him to furnish a story a week at one hundred dollars a story, he was successfully launched upon his career. This amazing pace, which began in December 1903, was sustained by O. Henry throughout the whole of 1904-5 and continued into 1906. These stories were the product of his New York environment. Before securing his contract with the *World*, he had frequently written about the Southwest or Latin America. Now he turned his energies to picturing the New York in which he lived.

O. Henry had begun his connection with the *New York World* as a writer of introductions for the feature sec-

tion. F. L. H. Noble, the Sunday editor of the *World,*
gave Robert H. Davis the assignment of finding O. Henry
and securing his services.[4] Davis was authorized to make
an offer of forty dollars a week, but if refused, he was
to increase it to a maximum of sixty. With only the
vague information that O. Henry lived somewhere on
West Twenty-fourth Street over a French restaurant, he
began a room-to-room search of the buildings in the
neighborhood and finally located Porter in a tiny hall
bedroom on the fourth floor of the Hotel Marty. Without
delay Davis made his best proposition first. O. Henry
accepted, and the whole transaction was completed in
less than five minutes.

O. Henry's employment by the *World* was almost
equally brief, for when Noble retired as Sunday editor,
his services also were terminated. However, when Bob
Davis later became fiction editor of the Frank A. Munsey
publications, he made a five-year contract with O. Henry
for the first reading of his entire output. In January 1905,
O. Henry agreed with Davis that in return for the privi-
lege of a first reading of his stories he was to receive ten
cents a word for all material accepted. Under this ar-
rangement some of his stories brought him as much as
five hundred dollars, but the usual income was from
about two hundred and fifty to three hundred and fifty
dollars per story.[5]

William Johnston was one of the many editors who
knew O. Henry. For three years Johnston had the task of
extracting stories from him, stories for which he had

already been paid but was not in the mood to write. As time went on, these moods became more frequent with O. Henry, yet he would promise to deliver a story, even though he knew he would be late in keeping his commitment. It was Johnston's job to prod him until the manuscript was delivered. When he was seeking a story, Johnston went to lunch with O. Henry and then to dinner, after which he followed him about during the evening, continuing his persistent pleading until the story was delivered. Always there was some excuse for his tardiness. Perhaps he had been bothered by "Colonel Bright and his justly celebrated disease," perhaps it had been "dizziness on rising," or it may have been some visitor who had stayed too long. Sometimes he would not even attempt an excuse, but would whimsically write:

What you say? Let's take an evening off and strike the Cafe Francis for a slight refection. I like to be waked up suddenly there by the music and look across at the red-haired woman eating smelts under an original by Glackens.

Peace for yours,
S. P.[6]

On another occasion he explained his lateness in delivering a story simply by saying, "Being entirely out of tune with the Muse, I went out and ameliorated the condition of a shop girl as far as a planked steak, etc. could do so." All of this sometimes became exasperating, and once Johnston wrote him: "He never kept a promise in his life." To this O. Henry replied:

Guilty, m'lud.

And yet—

Sometime ago a magazine editor to whom I had promised a story at a certain minute (and strangely enough didn't get there with it) wrote to me: "I am coming down to-morrow and kick you thoroughly with a pair of heavy-soled shoes. *I* never go back on *my* promises." And I lifted up my voice and said unto him: "It's easy to keep promises that can be pulled off with your feet."[7]

While serving as taskmaster, Johnston came to know him well. O. Henry appeared to him a shy, whimsical, gentle, and modest person, but seldom did he feel that he had penetrated the reserve with which Porter cloaked himself. "Indeed," wrote Johnston, "each time I read some new recollection of an 'intimate friend of O. Henry's,' I always picture his ghost sitting somewhere over a celestial highball—they must have highballs there or it wouldn't be heaven for him—smiling sarcastically. For Sydney Porter, gentle, lovable, talented though he was, had no intimate friends."[8]

Witter Bynner knew him fairly well, however, and, during the association which lasted between them for four years, became familiar with O. Henry's method of writing. His custom was to compose in his head an entire story, which he related to Bynner before reluctantly turning to the task of setting it down on paper. While O. Henry sat writing, Bynner would lie upon a couch, patiently waiting for the long-overdue story. It was Bynner who conceived the idea of weaving the O. Henry stories into the form of a novel, and convinced the McClure people that such a book would sell.[9] Owen Wister had successfully achieved this with *The Virginian,* and McClure believed that O. Henry could duplicate the process with his Central American writings. Convinced of the soundness of the idea and not wishing to refuse an attractive offer, he made the necessary changes in his stories, wrote three new chapters, and turned out the cleverly devised *Cabbages and Kings.*[10]

Although O. Henry lived at several different addresses in New York, the one that deserves to be called his home is 55 Irving Place, where he resided during his most prolific period. At present the room in which he wrote is occupied by a restaurant, but the old four-story brownstone house with its original entrance is easily recognizable. The large window through which he looked upon the street still covers the front of the first-floor room. It is but a few steps to the corner of Irving Place and Eighteenth Street, where the saloon of "The Lost Blend" still stands, looking almost exactly as described in the story:

The saloon (whether blessed or cursed) stood in one of those little "places" which are parallelograms instead of streets, and inhabited by laundries, decayed Knickerbocker families and Bohemians who have nothing to do with either.[11]

The saloon of "The Lost Blend" served as a club for the neighborhood. It was an intimate, quiet, orderly place, where the residents of the locality gathered in the evening for companionship. O. Henry was a regular visitor. There is the bar where Con "worked on the sober side," while "you and I stood, one-legged like geese, on the other side and went into voluntary liquidation with our week's wages."[12] There is the back room where the experiments were conducted in search of the "distilled elixir of battle, money, and high life," of which the author said, ". . . did you ever put on a straw hat with a yellow band around it and go up in a balloon with a pretty girl, with $8,000,000 in your pocket all at the same time? That's what thirty drops of it would make you feel like."[13]

O. Henry's life in New York taught him much, widened his range of vision, and quickened his sympathies for the ways of those who lived there. At any hour of the day or night he walked along the river fronts, through what was then known as Hell's Kitchen, or along the Bowery. Dropping into all manner of places, he talked to a diversity of people, especially the two kinds that seemed to interest him most: those who were in difficulty and those who were under a delusion. Restaurants of all varieties became his favorite haunts. He would sit night after night as an interested spectator, absorbing the atmosphere he later used in his stories, or roam at leisure from cheap café to saloon and back again, drawing directly from reality.

Thus, observing at first hand the byways of Manhattan, he was able to write stories with a firm knowledge of the underworld. It was a time when the city was undergoing an era of reform, and political intrigue and lawlessness furnished colorful excitement. Gangsters from the Bowery, toughs from Hell's Kitchen, ladies of pleasure from the dance halls, all furnished him with material. He knew the "sports" who talked glibly of the race track and the prize ring. He saw the inside of the "clubs" where illegal boxing bouts were held in stuffy, overcrowded rooms in squalid side streets. He knew likewise the aristocracy of gangdom, the wealthy leaders of the underworld who controlled the gunmen and the lesser criminals. He knew the inhabitants of the drab Sixth Avenue district, which was correctly termed "Satan's Circus." The conversation of these people, their mannerisms, their appearance, and their habits became a part of the things he wrote about. O. Henry always contended that he could go anywhere with impunity if he sat quietly by himself and refrained from bothering anyone or interfering with the other patrons.[14]

O. Henry once explained how he would spend his time if he could arrange it: An evening of dining "rather in style" at Mouquin's or the Café Francis would be followed the next day by a visit to the lower East Side, where he could "watch the police break into joints and get the 'local color.' " Then he would be in the mood to lock the door and spend an evening with one of Clark Russell's sea yarns. But the next night, after the theater, there would be a visit to a dance hall, where in a corner with somebody, he could listen to "THINGS!—the things that make literature if only the editors should let us write 'em." But the next evening, he said, "I'd be a direct

descendant of my Puritan ancestors—I'd write letters to
my relatives and read Macaulay's Essays."[15]

William Wash Williams has told us of the visits he and
O. Henry made to the rathskeller of Koster and Bial's
Café on Sixth Avenue, which served as a place of rendez-
vous for the prostitutes from the old Tenderloin section.
The two friends enjoyed gathering several of the girls at
a table and talking with them while they listened to the
singing waiters and a violinist who had seen better days.
One night when Williams happened to drop into the place
alone for a glass of beer, one of the girls startled him
with an inquiry about his "nut friend." When Williams
rather indignantly replied that his friend was no "nut,"
the girl confided to him that although this unusual person
never offered to take any of them out, he always paid
them for their time by slipping each girl some money
under the table. The whole situation which had the girls
so puzzled was to Williams typical of the man.[16]

On other evenings he attended the theater or strolled
along Broadway, never missing an opportunity to chat
with a communicative policeman. Walking over to Third
Avenue, he would let his imagination have full play, so
that a German restaurant called Scheffel Hall became the
Old Munich which formed the setting for "The Hal-
berdier of the Little Rheinschloss."[17] From there he might
continue to the Hotel America on Fifteenth Street, just a
short distance east of Fourth Avenue, where the clientele
had all the appearance of the *señors* and *capitans* that he

pictured in his stories of Latin revolutionaries.[18] Then he might wander to the entirely different atmosphere of the brownstone mansions, those residences of wealth inhabited by people he liked to call the Caliphs. Before ending the evening, he might by contrast watch the dock hands on the North River pier.

At other times he lounged on a Madison Square bench, where he could divide his attention between the park dwellers and the statue of Diana, which he so often mentioned in his writings. Perhaps he went to Coney Island to see the varied wonders which found their way into such stories as "Tobin's Palm." O. Henry did not confine himself to any one section of New York; he was interested in it all. And because he so saturated himself with its atmosphere, it appears vividly in his stories. His statement that his plots could happen anywhere does not mean that their background might be anywhere. It is New York and nowhere else in the world.

The beginning of the twentieth century in New York was the special era of the roof gardens, and O. Henry, a frequent visitor, preserved their atmosphere in several of his stories. To these places many of his characters went seeking adventure and escape from the drabness of their existence. People who could not afford such pleasure denied themselves for weeks to enjoy one evening of luxury. "Turning the tables on Haroun al Raschid," as O. Henry put it, they visited the haunts of the rich, disguised as wealthy men and women.[19] These excursions into a dream world furnished their only pleasure in life. In "While the Auto Waits," "The Caliph and the Cad," and "Lost on Dress Parade," his characters, like Browning's Pippa, spend the one day allotted to them for pleasure in forgetting their labors by fancying themselves in a higher station. Typical was Towers Chandler, who at the end of every ten weeks "purchased one gentleman's evening from the bargain counter of stingy old Father Time."[20]

In "Transients in Arcadia" O. Henry used as his background a Broadway hotel. He described its broad staircases, the aerial elevators gliding upward, carrying guests attended by guides in brass buttons, the lofty dining room with its cool twilight, where one dined at a snowy table on seafood "that would turn Old Point Comfort—'by Gad, sah!'—green with envy," or ate venison "that would melt the official heart of a game warden." Watchful waiters "supplying every want before it is expressed," a temperature of "perpetual April," the distant roar of Broadway transformed to a pleasing murmur—all this beneath a painted sky, "across which delicate clouds drift and do not vanish as those of nature do to our regret," completes O. Henry's accurate description.[21] Yet he could do equal justice to Bogle's Chop House and Family Restaurant, or the café patronized by Soapy in "The Cop and the Anthem," whose "crockery and atmosphere were thick; its soup and napery thin."[22]

He wrote of Gramercy Park and placed the residences of some of his characters there, making it the home of

the Van der Ruyslings of "The Discounters of Money,"
an aristocratic old family which received the first key
ever made to Gramercy Park. Also figuring in the
stories is Union Square, where one may still take a
seat on the third bench to the right as one enters the
square from the east, at the walk opposite the fountain,
and occupy the same place that Stuffy Pete did when
he met the old gentleman in "Two Thanksgiving Day
Gentlemen." "The Furnished Room" was located in
Greenwich Village and there, too, lived Hettie, who provided the beef for the Irish stew in "The Third Ingredient," and old Behrman, of "The Last Leaf." "The
Badge of Policeman O'Roon" takes the reader to Central Park, and "A Harlem Tragedy" to that section of
the city. Other localities and landmarks take their places
in the narratives—the clock tower at Madison Square,
the gilded statue of Diana watching over her wooded
park, the Statue of Liberty, the Flatiron Building loom-
ing mistily at night as it seemed to split the streets, "the
corner of the square presided over by George the
Veracious,"[23] the lower East Side, where in "The Social
Triangle" ragged children play in the streets, and the
ash cans and pushcarts clutter the pathways.

O. Henry's art was more than factual, however, for
as he himself put it: "If you have the right kind of eye
—the kind that can disregard high hats, cutaway coats,
and trolley cars—you can see all the characters in the
'Arabian Nights' parading up and down Broadway at
mid-day."[24] Ever alive to impressions, he was able to

see the city in all the glamour and brilliant hue of the
Bagdad of oriental imagination. In the prelude which
forms the opening paragraphs of "The Green Door,"
O. Henry said:

"In the big city the twin spirits Romance and Adventure are always abroad seeking worthy wooers . . . at
every corner handkerchiefs drop, fingers beckon, eyes
besiege, and the lost, the lonely, the rapturous, the mys-
terious, the perilous changing clues of adventure are
slipped into our fingers. . . . We pass on; and some day
we come, at the end of a very dull life, to reflect that
our romance has been a pallid thing of a marriage or
two, a satin rosette kept in a safe-deposit drawer, and a
lifelong feud with a steam radiator."

His interest in the theater and the people of its profession naturally led him to make the acquaintance of a
number of actors. Archibald Sessions has recounted an
evening which he and O. Henry spent at Miner's old
Eighth Avenue Theater, where one of the numbers on
the program was a trapeze act by a girl.[25] The climax
of the act occurred when the girl, swinging far out over
the audience, kicked off her garter. On that particular
evening it fell in O. Henry's lap. Although Sessions
has not said whether they met the actress, the story
which grew out of the incident, "The Memento," contains such realistic conversation there can be no doubt
that O. Henry knew someone like her. Rosalie Ray, the
heroine, candidly says, "The men I'd known come at
you with either diamonds, knock-out drops, or a raise of

salary—and their ideals! well we'll say no more."[26] From the time that she "settles herself with a skilful wriggle" on the top of a trunk until she asks in the closing sentence, "Is there any of that cocktail left, Lynn?" she is vividly before us, and her "You're damn right," hurled at the astonished landlady in the poky little village, carries all the conviction of actual conversation. At times he has revealing flashes of cynicism, and when he writes, "You hear a lot of sympathy sloshed around on chorus girls and their fifteen dollars a week. Piffle! There ain't a sorrow in the chorus that a lobster cannot heal,"[27] one feels that O. Henry knew his show girls.

Another of his heroines, Ida Bates of "The Enchanted Profile," was not a stenographer at all, but a chorus girl who had enjoyed a highly exciting career.[28] Perhaps she furnished the model for the actress of "Thimble, Thimble." Margaret Anglin was one of his theatrical acquaintances, and O. Henry was invited to a dinner given in her honor when she was playing in William Vaughn Moody's *The Great Divide*. As Al Jennings was visiting O. Henry on that evening, he was included as one of the guests. When asked for his opinion of the play, Jennings amused everybody by his realistic criticism.[29]

O. Henry enjoyed companionship, but he did not like large gatherings. He avoided literary meetings and celebrity hunters, preferring the company of his own selected friends. With one of these, Mabel Wagnalls, he carried on a delightful correspondence. Miss Wagnalls, daughter of the publisher, received several visits from O. Henry, whom she found less jocose in his conversation than in his writing; she has recalled only one witticism by him during his visits. Yet the letters he wrote her, which she published as *Letters to Lithopolis,* are full of fun and good jokes, with amusing sketches. Sometimes O. Henry was quiet and serious, and once he said to her with a tone of sadness, "Poverty is so terrible and so common, we should all do more than we do— much more—to relieve it."[30] There can be no doubt about his sincere sympathy for those who needed help, but were unable to help themselves. Stories like "Brickdust Row" and "An Unfinished Story" caused Theodore Roosevelt to say, "It was O. Henry who started me on my campaign for office girls."[31]

Because of this interest in the unfortunate, especially the victims of environment, the stories of O. Henry take on a sociological import. He presented the shopgirl, the derelict, the woman of the street, the gangster, against the background that produced them. He knew that environment can cause tragedy, and he realized the injustice of a system which would permit an employer to pay a clerk only six dollars a week. While dining on a cool and comfortable roof garden, one of his characters reproves another, "You might think about the kids down in Delancey and Hester streets lying out on the fire-escapes with their tongues hanging out, trying to get a breath of air that hasn't been fried on both sides.

The contrast might increase your enjoyment."[32] "Brick-dust Row" depicts the damaging effects on the lives of those whose surroundings are inadequate and squalid. "The Guilty Party" attempts to show that slum children, forced to play in the streets, are defeated in life before they start. It was in behalf of the shopgirl, however, that O. Henry finally dipped his pen in acid. "An Unfinished Story" ends with the author, at the bar of judgment, being asked if he belongs with a certain group:

"Who are they?" I asked.

"Why," said he, "they are the men who hired working-girls, and paid 'em five or six dollars a week to live on. Are you one of the bunch?"

"Not on your immortality," said I. "I'm only the fellow that set fire to an orphan asylum, and murdered a blind man for his pennies."[33]

In the same story the room which is occupied by Dulcie takes an active part in shaping the narrative, while in "The Furnished Room" the room itself becomes more prominent than the characters, its pervasive and compelling influence finally emerging above all else. "The Brief Debut of Tildy" is permeated by the atmosphere of a cheap restaurant. "The Third Ingredient" describes with equally accurate detail the poorer class of rooming house, the kind made from the joining of two old-fashioned, brownstone-front residences. So well has he related how Hettie cooked in her room that he must have known from experience how it was done. Air-shaft apartments, skylight rooms, parlor bedrooms—all of these he delineated with the touch of one who has seen them and has sympathy for their occupants.

The most characteristic element in O. Henry's plot construction is the surprise ending. It was not his invention, but he used it until it became familiarly associated with his name. Lesser writers have sought to imitate O. Henry, making use of trick endings which are cheap and illogical, but the surprise achieved by O. Henry is no trick. It is the valid and inevitable finish that the reader should have expected all along. O. Henry's friend W. W. Williams once asked him about the "snappers" at the end of the stories; O. Henry replied that often he began a story without knowing how it was going to end, that sometimes he saw straight through to the finish, and that occasionally he developed the narrative to fit a preconceived ending.[34] In each instance, however, the characters react to the situation consistently, and the laws of dramatic logic, as well as the traits of human nature, are never disregarded.

About this time, O. Henry revived an old friendship from his days in Austin. Mrs. Nettie Roach Daily, Athol's half sister, had come to New York, where she and O. Henry met again and became very good friends. During this period O. Henry's daughter, now a young lady, was attending what is today Ward-Belmont School in Nashville. Her Aunt Nettie often bought feminine things for her at the request of her father, who appreciated her interest in Margaret and was happy to have someone in whom he could confide. They were often together, sometimes every evening for a week, dining each night at a different restaurant, and then attending the theater. On such evenings O. Henry would provide his guest beforehand with flowers, candy, and perfumes.[35] This friendship came at the time O. Henry was at the height of his fame and not long before his second marriage.

The year 1904 is important in his life, for his first book, *Cabbages and Kings,* appeared then. It was likewise the first year of his contract with the *New York Sunday World Magazine,* to which he had begun to contribute in December 1903.[36] Moreover, in that year he signed all of his stories "O. Henry." As to the origin of his pen name he himself gave several different versions.[37] There seems no reason to reject the explanation given by C. Alphonso Smith that Porter found his pen name in the *United States Dispensatory,* which was the daily consulted reference work of every American drug clerk and in which the name of the celebrated French pharmacist, Etienne-Ossian Henry, appeared abbreviated to O. Henry.[38]

The years 1904 and 1905 were the most prolific. His second book, *The Four Million,* which appeared in 1906, was composed of the stories from this period; all but two of the twenty-five stories in the volume were written then. In his prefatory note to the collection, O. Henry stated:

Not very long ago some one invented the assertion that there were only "Four Hundred" people in New York City who were

really worth noticing. But a wiser man has arisen—the census
taker—and his larger estimate of human interest has been preferred in marking out the field of these little stories of the
"Four Million."[39]

With his second volume O. Henry established himself
as a writer of distinction. *The Four Million* represents
some of his finest work; it contains the stories which
have been the most popular and are most frequently
associated with his name. With their publication in book
form O. Henry became the acknowledged portrayer of
the life of New York City. What Page was to Virginia,
Cable to New Orleans, and Craddock to the Tennessee
mountains, O. Henry was to the great metropolis in the
eyes of millions of readers. In 1907 he added another
volume, *The Trimmed Lamp,* which contained some of
his best stories of New York, and in the same year appeared *Heart of the West,* a collection of stories based
on his experiences in Texas. If these two volumes did
not measure up to *The Four Million,* they were nevertheless entertaining and popular, a permanent picture of
the times they delineate.

In the spring of 1905, O. Henry had received a letter
from Sallie Coleman, whom he had known in Greensboro, asking if the author of "Madame Bo-Peep of the
Ranches" might be Will Porter. O. Henry's reply re-
opened a youthful friendship which progressed to the
stage of courtship.

With the success achieved from his writing, Porter
now felt himself financially able to marry again, and

Miss Coleman's visit to New York while making a trip to Boston did the trick. She has told the story herself: "How I did enjoy my stay! I certainly had a heavenly time. Will showed me the sights of the city, and never was there a more perfect self-appointed cruise conductor. As you may guess, we were engaged before I left New York."[40]

Shortly before the wedding, O. Henry wrote Gilman Hall, telling him that "the hullabaloo will occur" at Wynn Cottage. He requested several favors of his friend: "Please go to Tiffany's and get a wedding ring, size $5\frac{1}{8}$. Sara says the bands worn now are quite narrow— and that's the kind she wants." Also, he asked for ". . . a couple of dress collars, size $16\frac{1}{2}$." Finally he asked Hall to buy two bouquets, one of lilies of the valley, the other of pale pink roses.[41]

They were married in Asheville, November 27, 1907, the Reverend R. F. Campbell performing the ceremony. The minister, wishing to be sure that everything progressed smoothly, took care to send detailed instructions to O. Henry by his best man, Gilman Hall. When Hall started to go through the list of what the groom was expected to do, O. Henry replied: "Look here, Gilman, you and that preacher needn't try to rattle me. I have a ring in every pocket."[42] After the wedding the couple left for Hot Springs, where they spent their honeymoon at a winter resort hotel deep in the mountains. The future as they planned it then looked bright and happy.

Because of his work, the Porters soon returned to New

York. With a wife and a grown daughter to support, O. Henry was faced with the necessity of producing stories whether he felt like it or not. According to Mrs. Porter, they lived at the Chelsea, an old family hotel between Seventh and Eighth Avenue on West Twenty-third Street,[43] and spent the summer on Long Island, where Margaret lived with them. The relationship between Margaret and O. Henry was more like that of two good friends than one of father and daughter. Margaret said in later years that not once did her father ever give her a command, yet she did not think of doing anything other than what he wished her to do. Her memories of her father are of particular interest.[44] Sitting at the piano, he would softly play the accompaniment to some gay "darky" song, and with only Margaret for an audience, he would sing it to her in dialect. If another person should happen to intrude, he would become silent at once. In one of his lighter moods one evening he brought home a guitar and a mandolin and entertained the family with an evening of song. Another time, after dinner, he amused the household with impersonations of famous people. Margaret recalled how she and her father liked to take walks together, sometimes going on hunting trips, during which O. Henry would carry a gun but never use it except to shoot at targets; he derived no pleasure from killing any animal.

In the fall of 1908, O. Henry brought his family back into the city, taking an apartment down in Greenwich Village, where they stayed for several months. It was a rather expensive apartment in Waverly Place, renting for one hundred dollars a month.[45] After leaving this residence, he spent a good deal of time alone in New York, while Mrs. Porter returned to North Carolina. They made frequent trips back and forth, and occasionally O. Henry came to New York alone to work, returning to his old haunts and taking up his old ways again. During this year appeared *The Voice of the City*, a volume containing some of his best stories, and *The Gentle Grafter*, of interest for the pictures it gives of medicine men, street fakers, and small-time swindlers.

On April 4, 1909, the *New York Sunday Times* carried an interview with O. Henry by George MacAdam, the only one O. Henry ever gave.[46] In talking to MacAdam, he was careful to set the date of his birth as 1867, to be sure that the years covering his prison experiences were omitted. As he was not interested in perpetuating the current myths about himself, he confided that he had never seen a mine in his life, that the closest he had ever come to being a tintype artist was having his picture taken with his arm draped gracefully over a lady's shoulder, and that he had never ridden a mile except in a Pullman. The years he wished to conceal he glossed over by recounting a plausible story of a trip to Central America to go into the fruit business. He abandoned his fruit plantation, he said, because of a shortage of funds, and drifted back to Texas. He finished the tale by saying that he finally went to New Orleans, where he began his literary career in earnest.

Making no mystery about his method of writing, he confided that he always tried to get the story complete and well in mind before he attempted to touch pencil to paper. Once the story was under way, he finished it quickly and mailed it to an editor without revising. He admitted having dry spells, periods during which he could not write a line, which sometimes lasted for as long as three months. When these unproductive periods were upon him, he would quit trying to write. "You can't write a story that's got any life in it by sitting at a writing table and thinking," he said. "You've got to get out into the streets, into the crowds, talk with people, and feel the rush and throb of real life—that's the stimulant for a story writer."[47] When the interview was over and MacAdam had handed him the written account, O. Henry read it through twice. Then without offering to change a word, he returned it to the reporter with the simple comment, "You seem to have got me," whereupon he and his interviewer adjourned to one of his favorite haunts for talk and refreshment, and no more was said upon the subject.

Harry Peyton Steger often worked with O. Henry at the Caledonia Hotel, where he frequently stayed when writing. Steger said that O. Henry did all of his writing on small yellow sheets with a carbon copy. During these final years in New York Steger acted as paymaster as well as friend and companion to him, and later was guardian to Margaret.[48] He was under the impression that O. Henry gave his money away, for he would sometimes receive three hundred dollars, and in only about two days would request two hundred more. Franklin P. Adams, who also had occasion to observe O. Henry's financial habits, told Arthur W. Page that at one time he lent O. Henry eight hundred dollars and that at another time the debt amounted to sixteen hundred dollars. It was repaid, however, and Adams felt that much of O. Henry's money went to pay for Margaret's schooling.[49]

It seems unnecessary to look for obscure reasons for O. Henry's frequent financial embarrassments. Although there is the possibility of blackmail, it is easy enough to account for his need for money on more probable grounds. He was always generously helping others, and he never stopped to count the cost. His young friend, W. W. Williams, was once hard pressed for money, and O. Henry insisted upon paying his room and board for him. When Williams expressed his embarrassment about accepting assistance, O. Henry replied, ". . . it is my place to do just what I did tonight . . . take the situation in my own hands and pull you out of the hole. And if at any time the conditions are turned around I know you would come to me the same way. Bill, if friendship doesn't mean that, it doesn't mean anything."[50]

A discussion of O. Henry as a man or writer would be incomplete without some reference to his efforts as a playwright.[51] For some time he had wanted to try his hand at writing for the stage and now with his need for

additional income he naturally turned to the theater as
a quick means of securing it. He decided to collaborate
with Franklin P. Adams on the libretto for a musical
comedy call *Lo,* the music to be furnished by A. Baldwin
Sloane. It was based on O. Henry's story "To Him
Who Waits," and derived its title from Pope's "Lo, the
poor Indian. . . ." *Lo* was produced in Aurora, Illinois,
in August 1909, played single night stands in Waukegan
and Janesville, followed by a week in Milwaukee, and
breathed its last in St. Joseph, Missouri. It lasted four-
teen weeks in all and O. Henry did not see a single
performance.

The failure of *Lo,* however, did not dampen his hopes
of ultimate success. A friend, Campbell MacCulloch,
later a motion picture executive, was at that time employed in the business side of the theatrical profession
in New York. Through him O. Henry met George C.
Tyler, the theatrical producer, whom MacCulloch had
impressed with the dramatic possibilities of "A Retrieved Reformation." When Tyler asked O. Henry to
make a version for stage production, he agreed. The
play was not forthcoming, however, and Tyler, after
waiting for some time, became impatient to get the production under way. He wired O. Henry an offer of five
hundred dollars for the stage rights to his story, which
the latter accepted. An adaptation was made by Paul
Armstrong, a clever craftsman, under the title *Alias
Jimmy Valentine* and produced with H. B. Warner and
Laurette Taylor in the leading roles. When O. Henry

learned that Armstrong had earned more than a hundred thousand dollars for his adaptation, he determined to write a play. His two volumes of short stories published in 1909, *Roads of Destiny* and *Options,* although quite creditable and containing some of his best writing, had yielded him nothing compared with the royalties Armstrong was receiving.

Stimulated by the desire for a similar success, O. Henry wrote Tyler from Asheville during the early part of 1910. He promised to come to New York, hide himself away, keep his whereabouts a secret from everybody but Tyler, and start work upon a play. Requesting an advance of five hundred dollars to enable him to reach the city, he offered to make over to Tyler the dramatic rights to all his stories until this particular work was done. On January 25, 1910, O. Henry wrote again, saying that he needed five hundred dollars for the payment of debts and promising to arrive in New York within the next week if he received seven hundred and fifty dollars by wire.[52] His unusual offer to give Tyler his exclusive services and the future rights to all his stories in advance shows that he was badly in need of cash.

The same desperate need is revealed by his correspondence with his publishers. Nearly a year before, he had written to them asking for advances on the novel which he hoped to commence. March 16, 1909, found him writing to H. W. Lanier of Doubleday, Page and Company, saying, "In a short time—say two weeks at the outside—I'll turn in enough of the book for the pur-

poses you require, as per your last letter."[53] In this same
letter, O. Henry assured Lanier that his collaboration
with Adams on *Lo* would take no time from his work on
this project. Yet if he ever produced anything on the
novel for which he had asked Lanier for advances, nobody has recorded seeing it.

During the last year of his life he was desperately
trying to increase his earning power. In March 1910,
Strictly Business appeared, containing "A Municipal
Report," generally looked upon as one of his finest creations. This was the last of his books to be published during his lifetime. In addition to his efforts as a playwright and as a novelist, he wrote six stories and two
poems which were printed in the magazines in 1910.[54]
This task of writing was made still more difficult by
frequent occurrences of ill health. He went to Asheville
and joined his wife and daughter. Setting up an office
on the fifth floor of a Patton Avenue building, he tried
to carry on his work, but was unable to accomplish anything important. In November, after suffering a slight
relapse, he appeared to be much better, and by March of
the following year he was once more in New York.
Again he found himself unable to work and for the next
month spent most of the time in bed. His nerves were
shattered, and he was unable to continue the task which
had brought him back to the city.

The writing of a play based on his story "The World
and the Door" had to wait. Vainly he strove to get himself in shape. During the last month of his life in New

York he became a hermit and, according to Will Irwin, shut himself up and kept the telephone off the hook.[55] Just what happened during these last days before he was carried to the Polyclinic Hospital, nobody really knows, but nine empty whiskey bottles were found under his bed.[56] C. Alphonso Smith states that Gilman Hall had him removed to the hospital,[57] but Dr. Charles Russell Hancock, the physician, declared that Anne Partlan called him to attend O. Henry. At any rate, only the doctor was with him when he died. The *New York Tribune* for June 6, 1910, carried an account of O. Henry's death, attributing the cause to cirrhosis of the liver and quoting the doctor: "His liver was all wrong, his digestion was shattered, his nerves were in a terrible condition, and his heart was too weak to stand the shock."[58] In more than a full column devoted to O. Henry's death, the *New York Times* on the same date printed the doctor's statement that O. Henry, who was conscious at the end, died from a complication of diseases and not from an operation. No operation, indeed, was performed.

The story of his death has been often told: how he asked for more light that he might not go home in the dark, giving a new meaning to the jest of a popular song. His funeral was held in the Little Church Around the Corner. Franklin P. Adams was in charge of arrangements, and among the pallbearers were Will Irwin and Richard Harding Davis.[59] There was an O. Henryesque touch to the funeral. By mistake a wedding had been scheduled for the same time, and the gay party was forced to wait while services were performed for the narrator of *The Four Million.* He was buried in Asheville, North Carolina, where the grave is marked by a simple granite block bearing the inscription: "William Sydney Porter 1862-1910."

After O. Henry's death, *Whirligigs* (1910) appeared; it contained "The Ransom of Red Chief," generally acclaimed the funniest of all O. Henry's tales. Some of his finest prose appears in "Blind Man's Holiday," and other stories in this volume like "A Blackjack Bargainer," "The Roads We Take," and "Georgia's Ruling" have real merit. "The Song and the Sergeant" is an interesting account of the theatrical profession, and "One Dollar's Worth" is an example of the popular type of Western yarn at its best.

Sixes and Sevens (1911) includes a good story of Texas in "The Last of the Troubadours," and an accurate and amusing account of a holdup, "Holding Up a Train," was actually told to O. Henry by Al Jennings. "The Champion of the Weather" is a humorous account of a cowboy's experiences in New York, while "Let Me Feel Your Pulse" and "A Ghost of a Chance" help round out a volume that is entertaining and lively.

Though containing a few good stories, such as "A Fog in Santone" and "The Marionettes," *Rolling Stones* (1912) is made up for the most part of caricatures and slight sketches written in O. Henry's early years, and the volume as a whole detracts from his reputation. *Waifs and Strays* (1917) is a better collection, but once again there is nothing to be compared with O. Henry at his best. *O. Henryana* (1920), a collection of seven poems and short sketches, was published in a limited edition. "The Crucible" is O. Henry's best effort in verse, and "The Elusive Tenderloin" is of interest as his first short story written for the *New York Sunday World*. Another limited edition, *Letters to Lithopolis* (1922), contains a series of interesting and amusing letters from O. Henry to Mabel Wagnalls. *Postscripts* (1923) is a volume of sketches written for the *Houston Post*. Though interesting to the student of O. Henry, it contains nothing of any importance as an example of his art. A second collection of these sketches, *O. Henry Encore* (1939), which contains some interesting writing suggestive of his later powers, rounds out the publication of his early work.

His books have sold literally by the millions throughout the world, more than five million copies having been purchased in the United States.[60] He has been translated into French, German, Spanish, Italian, Swedish, Dano-Norwegian, Japanese, Chinese, and Russian.[61] As much of his work is still read, the really fine stories should become a permanent addition to American literature. In them O. Henry not only widened the experience of his readers, he restated the verities which exist wherever people continue to strive for truth and beauty in life. He was never unsympathetic, except with those who sought to deprive others of their rights as human beings, and his writings have in them feelings of compassion for the weakness of man, which, joined with his remarkable ability of expression, make his stories at their best an influence for the furthering of those ideals which still tend to command the allegiance of civilized men.

Notes

CHAPTER II:

1. C. Alphonso Smith, *O. Henry Biography*, p. 60, hereafter referred to as *Biography*.
2. Smith, *Biography*, p. 23.
3. *Ibid.*, p. 19.
4. *Ibid.*, p. 20.
5. Notes by C. Alphonso Smith from interviews. Now in the Greensboro Public Library, these notes will hereafter be referred to as Smith Notes.
6. Smith, *Biography*, pp. 33-38.
7. *Ibid.*, p. 30.
8. *Ibid.*, p. 44.
9. Statements of Mrs. J. K. Hall and Mrs. R. M. Hall, Smith Notes.
10. Smith Notes.
11. *Ibid.*
12. Statement of Bettie Caldwell, Smith Notes.
13. Tom Tate in June 1932 told the writer his memories of the Porter family.
14. Statement of O. Henry to Mrs. R. M. Hall, Smith Notes.
15. Told to the writer by Tom Tate.
16. Smith, *Biography*, pp. 77-78.
17. *Ibid.*, p. 69.
18. Told to the writer by Tom Tate.
19. Smith, *Biography*, p. 46.
20. *Ibid.*, p. 90.
21. *Ibid.*, p. 91.
22. *Ibid.*, p. 228.
23. *Ibid.*, p. 81.
24. *Ibid.*, p. 82.

25. *Ibid.*, p. 92.
26. *Ibid.*, p. 94.

CHAPTER III:

1. Letter to the writer from R. S. Henry of the American Association of Railroads, September 28, 1939.
2. MS letter in the Greensboro Public Library.
3. Lollie Cave Wilson, *Hard to Forget*, p. 1.
4. *The Complete Works of O. Henry* (one volume edition), p. 122.
5. Dora Neill Raymond, *Captain Lee Hall of Texas*, p. 191.
6. *A Vaquero of the Brush Country* (Dallas, 1929), p. 89.
7. Hyder E. Rollins, "O. Henry's Texas Days," *The Bookman*, XL (1914), 155.
8. Raymond, *op. cit.*, p. 193.
9. Rollins, "Texas Days," p. 156.
10. Mabel Wagnalls, *Letters to Lithopolis*, p. 2.
11. Smith, *Biography*, p. 99.
12. Raymond, *op. cit.*, p. 204. O. Henry has pictured the incident in his story "The Higher Abdication."
13. Robert H. Davis and Arthur B. Maurice, *The Caliph of Bagdad*, p. 300.
14. Al Jennings, *Through the Shadows with O. Henry*, p. 93.
15. Rollins, "Texas Days," p. 158.
16. *Ibid.*, p. 156.
17. MS letter in the Greensboro Public Library.
18. Smith, *Biography*, p. 101.
19. Rollins, "Texas Days," p. 158.
20. *Complete Works*, pp. 833-34.
21. O. Henry MSS in Greensboro Public Library.
22. *Ibid.*
23. *Ibid.*
24. Smith, *Biography*, p. 110.
25. *Ibid.*, p. 108.

26. *Complete Works*, p. 834.
27. MS letter in Greensboro Public Library.
28. Smith Notes.
29. MS letter from O. Henry to Mrs. Hall, March 13, 1884, in Greensboro Public Library. This passage was deleted by Smith in *Biography*, p. 114.
30. Smith seems to have feared someone might take this joke seriously and he deleted it from the letter in *Biography*, p. 113.
31. *Complete Works*, p. 173.
32. Rollins, "Texas Days," p. 158.
33. Smith, *Biography*, p. 106.
34. Wagnalls, *op. cit.*, p. 30.
35. P. 198.
36. See Florence Stratton and Vincent Burke, *The White Plume*.
37. *Complete Works*, p. 836.
38. *Ibid.*, p. 546.
39. Rollins, "Texas Days," p. 159.

CHAPTER IV:

1. Edmunds Travis, "O. Henry's Austin Years," *Bunker's Monthly*, I (1928), 495.
2. *Complete Works*, p. 546.
3. Travis, "Austin Years," p. 495.
4. *Ibid.*, p. 496.
5. Rollins, "Texas Days," p. 160.
6. The account of the quartet was told the writer by Hillyer in 1931.
7. *Complete Works*, p. 839.
8. Theater program in Smith Collection.
9. Wagnalls, *op. cit.*, p. 26.
10. Frances G. Maltby, *The Dimity Sweetheart*, p. 25.
11. Travis, "Austin Years," p. 499.

12. Arthur W. Page, "Little Pictures of O. Henry," *Complete Works*, p. 1327.

13. *Loc. cit.*

14. Wilson, *op. cit.*, p. 31.

15. *Ibid.*, p. 112.

16. *Ibid.*, p. 74.

17. Travis, "Austin Years," p. 501.

18. Rollins, "Texas Days," p. 161.

19. *Loc. cit.*

20. *Loc. cit.*

21. Travis, "Austin Years," p. 497.

22. Maltby, *op. cit.*, p. 17.

23. *Ibid.*, p. 7.

24. *Ibid.*, p. 11.

25. *Ibid.*, p. 9.

26. *Ibid.*, p. 26.

27. *Ibid.*, p. 34.

28. *Complete Works*, p. 65.

29. "Austin Homes of O. Henry," *The Texas Weekly*, VI (1930), 8.

30. Maltby, *op. cit.*, p. 39.

31. Paul S. Clarkson, *A Bibliography of William Sydney Porter (O. Henry)*, p. 8. See also Smith's *Biography*, pp. 122-23.

32. Smith, *Biography*, p. 124.

33. Travis, "Austin Years," p. 502.

34. Maltby, *op. cit.*, p. 42.

35. Travis, "Austin Years," p. 503.

36. *Loc. cit.*

37. Smith Notes.

38. Maltby, *op. cit.*, p. 46.

39. The writer has seen these letters but has been asked not to quote them or reveal the name of the family.

40. For an account of these illustrations, see W. D. Hornaday,

"Artists Were Scarce in O. Henry's Texas Days," *New York Times Book Review*, Jan. 3, 1926, p. 2.

41. Rollins, "Texas Days," p. 164.
42. A copy of this picture is in the Greensboro Public Library.
43. Reproduced in the *Dallas Morning News*, Feature Section, Feb. 12, 1933, p. 2.
44. Rollins, "Texas Days," p. 162.
45. Travis, "Austin Years," p. 504.
46. Rollins, "Texas Days," p. 162.
47. Maltby, *op. cit.*, p. 49.
48. Travis, "Austin Years," p. 506.
49. Rollins, "Texas Days," p. 163.
50. For a full account of these changes, see Fannie E. Ratchford, "The Rolling Stone: the Life History of an O. Henry Rarity," *The Colophon*, V: Part 17 (June 1934).
51. Rollins, "Texas Days," p. 163.
52. Harry Peyton Steger, Introduction to *Rolling Stones* (Biographical Ed.; New York, 1925), pp. xviii-xix.
53. *The Dallas Morning News*, Feature Section, August 9, 1931, p. 2.
54. Rollins, "Texas Days," p. 163.
55. C. Alphonso Smith in a letter to the *New York Times*, June 7, 1923, p. 18, col. 7, claimed that Porter used the name "O. Henry" in this issue of his paper. However, Fannie E. Ratchford and Ray Neumann, who have examined the copy, testify that it is not there. Perhaps it was used in another issue of *The Rolling Stone* which is now missing.
56. Rollins, "Texas Days," p. 165.
57. Smith, *Biography*, p. 129.
58. *Ibid.*, p. 130.
59. Florence Stratton, *Postscripts by O. Henry*, p. xvii.
60. *Ibid.*, p. xi.
61. Wilson, *op. cit.*, p. 156.

62. Indictment No. 1145, Austin Court Records.
63. Smith Notes.
64. Mary S. Harrell, *O. Henry Encore,* p. xiv.
65. Court Records, Austin, Texas.
66. Hyder E. Rollins, "Review of the Caliph of Bagdad," *Saturday Review of Literature,* VII (1931), 923.
67. *Loc. cit.*
68. Smith Notes.

CHAPTER V:

1. *Complete Works,* p. 951.
2. Wilson, *op. cit.,* p. 196.
3. Letter from J. M. Monget to C. A. Smith, Nov. 20, 1915, Smith Notes.
4. E. L. Tinker, "Why O. Henry," *The Bookman,* LXI (1925), 436.
5. Letter from F. Duval Armstrong to the writer, December 13, 1939.
6. Complete Works, p. 347.
7. *Ibid.,* p. 351.
8. Letter from F. D. Armstrong previously cited.
9. Jennings, *op. cit.,* p. 76. Jennings gives no dates, merely stringing out a romantic story of daredevil adventure.
10. *Complete Works,* p. 433.
11. Smith Notes.
12. Smith, *Biography,* p. 141.
13. Wilson, *op. cit.,* p. 198.
14. Smith, *Biography,* p. 142.
15. Rollins, "Review of the Caliph of Bagdad" *Saturday Review of Literature,* VII (1931), p. 923.
16. Printed transcript, *The United States* versus *W. S. Porter,* sent to the United States Circuit Court of Appeals in New Orleans, p. 6.

CHAPTER VI:

1. Edmunds Travis, "O. Henry Enters the Shadows," *Bunker's Monthly*, I (1928), 678.
2. Smith Notes.
3. Maltby, *op. cit.*, p. 71.
4. *Ibid.*, p. 74.
5. Smith Notes.
6. *Ibid.*
7. Letter to the writer from Edward G. Kemp, Assistant to the United States Attorney General, Oct. 5, 1939.
8. Statement of R. U. Culberson to C. A. Smith on Oct. 18, 1915, Smith Notes.
9. File No. 7243, 1891, of the Department of Justice, Washington, D. C., was made available to Luther W. Courtney through the courtesy of Senator Tom Connally. This file retains the confidential information sent to Washington by the bank examiners. See Courtney, "O. Henry's Case Reconsidered," *American Literature*, XIV (1943), 361-71.
10. "Review of O. Henry Biography," *The Nation*, CIV (1917), 52. Rollins herein pointed out the facts of the matter for the first time.
11. Austin Court Records. The three indictments, embodying only two charges, unfortunately led to a confused account of the proceedings by Smith in his *Biography*, pp. 136-46. Rollins noted this in *The Nation*, CIV (1917), 52, and in the *Saturday Review of Literature*, VII (1931), 922-23.
12. Filed February 1, 1897, and overruled by the Court on February 15, 1897, Printed transcript, *The United States versus W. S. Porter*, sent to the United States Circuit Court of Appeals in New Orleans, pp. 8-10.
13. Filed February 17, 1898, *ibid.*, p. 10.
14. *Ibid.*, p. 12.
15. *Ibid.*, pp. 13-14.

16. Austin Court Records.
17. *Ibid.*
18. *Ibid.*
19. Charge of the Court, filed February 17, 1898, Printed transcript, p. 15.
20. *Loc. cit.*
21. *Ibid.*, p. 16.
22. *Ibid.*, p. 19.
23. *Ibid.*, p. 20.
24. *Loc. cit.*
25. *Ibid.*, p. 23.
26. *Ibid.*, pp. 28-31.
27. *Ibid.*, p. 35.
28. Endorsement on the back of the printed transcript by G. L. Siebrecht.
29. Letter from the clerk of this court to the writer, September 15, 1939.
30. Courtney, *op. cit.*, p. 370.

CHAPTER VII:

1. Smith, *Biography*, p. 158.
2. *Ibid.*, p. 161.
3. *Ibid.*, p. 160.
4. *Ibid.*, p. 162.
5. *Ibid.*, p. 165.
6. *Ibid.*, p. 164.
7. *Ibid.*, p. 162.
8. Smith Notes.
9. Smith, *Biography*, p. 156.
10. *Ibid.*, pp. 154-57.
11. *Ibid.*, p. 170.
12. Letter from O. Henry to Mrs. Roach, November 5, 1900, in Greensboro Public Library.
13. Smith, *Biography*, pp. 157-58.

14. *Ibid.*, p. 146.
15. Smith Notes.

CHAPTER VIII:

1. Smith, *Biography*, p. 173.
2. "Little Pictures," p. 1331.
3. Davis and Maurice, *op. cit.*, p. 265.
4. *Ibid.*, p. 201. Davis' account is given in Chapter XIII.
5. *Ibid.*, p. 242.
6. William Johnston, "Disciplining O. Henry," *The Bookman*, LII (1921), 536.
7. *Loc. cit.*
8. *Loc. cit.*
9. Davis and Maurice, *op. cit.*, p. 267.
10. Paul S. Clarkson, "A Decomposition of Cabbages and Kings," *American Literature*, VII (1935), 195.
11. *Complete Works*, p. 1114.
12. *Loc. cit.*
13. *Ibid.*, p. 1115.
14. William Wash Williams, *The Quiet Lodger of Irving Place*, p. 133.
15. Letter to Ethel L. Patterson from O. Henry, quoted by Davis and Maurice, *op. cit.*, p. 280.
16. Williams, *op. cit.*, pp. 135-38.
17. Davis and Maurice, *op. cit.*, p. 327.
18. *Ibid.*, p. 338.
19. *Ibid.*, p. 721.
20. *Ibid.*, p. 72.
21. *Ibid.*, p. 1034.
22. *Ibid.*, p. 32.
23. *Ibid.*, p. 1163.
24. George MacAdam, "O. Henry's Only Autobiographia," *O. Henry Papers*, p. 21.

25. Archibald Sessions, "Some Odds and Ends about O. Henry," *Ainslee's*, XLVIII (1921), 150.
26. *Complete Works*, p. 1059.
27. *Ibid.*, p. 1058.
28. Davis and Maurice, *op. cit.*, p. 333.
29. Jennings, *op. cit.*, p. 303.
30. Wagnalls, *op. cit.*, p. xxiv.
31. Letter to C. A. Smith, reproduced in an advertisement, *The Mentor*, XI (1923), d.
32. *Complete Works*, p. 620.
33. *Ibid.*, p. 60.
34. Williams, *op. cit.*, p. 186.
35. Margetta Jung, "O. Henry in Manhattan," *Southwest Review*, XXIV (1939), 412.
36. Clarkson, *Bibliography*, p. 108. For a complete list of O. Henry's stories and the names signed to them, see "Periodical Appearances," pp. 101-11.
37. Paul S. Clarkson, "Whence 'O. Henry'?" *Saturday Review of Literature*, X (1934), 404.
38. C. Alphonso Smith, ed., *Selected Stories from O. Henry*, p. 91, See also Smith's "O. Henry," *The Nation*, CVI (1918), 567.
39. Preface to *The Four Million* (New York, 1906).
40. Ida Briggs Henderson, "The Courtship of O. Henry," *The State*, February 9, 1935, p. 8.
41. *Complete Works*, pp. 844-45.
42. Letter from the Reverend R. F. Campbell to C. A. Smith, October 5, 1915, Smith Notes.
43. Letter to the writer from Mrs. Porter, January 21, 1940.
44. Margaret Porter's memories of her father were printed in "My O. Henry," *The Mentor*, XI (1923), 17-20.
45. Letter from Mrs. Porter, *supra*.
46. Reprinted in *O. Henry Papers* (New York, 1924), pp. 5-25.

47. *Ibid.,* p. 20.
48. John A. Lomax, "Harry Steger and O. Henry," *Southwest Review,* XXIV (1939), 309.
49. Letter from A. W. Page to C. A. Smith, June 26, 1916, Smith Notes.
50. Williams, *op. cit.,* p. 223.
51. Alexander Woollcott, "O. Henry, Playwright," *Golden Book,* XIX (1934), 570-76.
52. *Ibid.,* p. 575.
53. Clarence Gohdes, "Some Letters by O. Henry," *South Atlantic Quarterly,* XXXVIII (1939), 35.
54. Clarkson, *Bibliography,* pp. 103-11.
55. "O. Henry, Man and Writer," *Cosmopolitan,* XLIX (1910), 447.
56. "Bob Davis Talks on 'The Caliph of Bagdad,' " *New York Times Book Review,* January 5, 1941, p. 2.
57. Smith, *Biography,* p. 249.
58. Newspaper clipping in Greensboro Public Library. See also *New York Times,* Monday, June 6, 1910, p. 7.
59. Davis and Maurice, *op. cit.,* p. 397.
60. Clarkson, *Bibliography,* p. 10.
61. C. Alphonso Smith, *Southern Literary Studies* (Chapel Hill, N. C., 1927), p. 158. See also A. Parry, "O. Henry Invades Russia," *The Mentor,* XV (1927), 38-39.

Selected Bibliography

Separate Works by O. Henry

Cabbages and Kings (1904).
The Four Million (1906).
The Trimmed Lamp (1907).
Heart of the West (1907).
The Voice of the City (1908).
The Gentle Grafter (1908).
Roads of Destiny (1909).
Options (1909).
Strictly Business (1910).
Whirligigs (1910).
Sixes and Sevens (1911).
Rolling Stones (1912).
Waifs and Strays (1917).
O. Henryana (1920).
Postscripts (1923).
O. Henry Encore (1939).

Collected Editions

O. Henry's Works, Authorized Edition; 12 vols. New York, 1913.
The Complete Writings of O. Henry, Memorial Edition; 14 vols. New York, 1917.
O. Henry, Biographical Edition; 18 vols. New York, 1925.
The Complete Works of O. Henry; 1 vol. New York, 1928.

Selected Editions

Selected Stories from O. Henry, edited by C. Alphonso Smith. New York, 1922.

Best Stories of O. Henry, edited by Bennett Cerf and Van H. Cartmell. New York, 1945.

Bibliographies

Clarkson, Paul S., *A Bibliography of William Sydney Porter (O. Henry).* Caldwell, Idaho, 1938.

O. Henry Papers, Containing Some Sketches of His Life together with an Alphabetical Index to His Complete Works. New York, 1924.

Literary History of the United States, edited by Robert E. Spiller *et al.,* III, 696-98. New York, 1948.

Authorized Biography

Smith, C. Alphonso, *O. Henry, Biography.* New York, 1916.

Supplementary Sources

Clarkson, Paul S., "A Decomposition of Cabbages and Kings," *American Literature,* VII (1935), 195-202.

————, "Whence 'O. Henry'?" *Saturday Review of Literature,* X (1934), 404.

Courtney, Luther W., "O. Henry's Case Reconsidered," *American Literature,* XIV (1943), 361-71.

Davis, Robert H., and Arthur B. Maurice, *The Caliph of Bagdad.* New York, 1931.

Firkins, O. W., "O. Henry" in *Modern Essays,* selected by Christopher Morley. New York, 1921.

Gohdes, Clarence, "Some Letters by O. Henry," *South Atlantic Quarterly,* XXXVIII (1939), 31-39.

Harrell, Mary S., *O. Henry Encore.* New York, 1939.

Henderson, Archibald, *O. Henry, a Memorial Essay.* Raleigh, North Carolina, 1914.

Irwin, Will, "O. Henry, Man and Writer," *Cosmopolitan,* XLIX (1910), 447.

Jennings, Al, *Through the Shadows with O. Henry*. New York, 1921.

Johnston, William, "Disciplining O. Henry," *The Bookman*, LII (1921), 536.

Jung, Margetta, "O. Henry in Manhattan," *Southwest Review*, XXIV (1939), 411-15.

Leacock, Stephen, "The Amazing Genius of O. Henry," *Essays and Literary Studies*. New York and London, 1916.

Lomax, John A., "Harry Steger and O. Henry," *Southwest Review*, XXIV (1939), 299-316.

MacAdam, George, "O. Henry's Only Autobiographia," *O. Henry Papers*. New York, 1924.

Mais, S. P. B., "O. Henry," *From Shakespeare to O. Henry*. London, 1917.

Maltby, Frances G., *The Dimity Sweetheart*. Richmond, Virginia, 1930.

Mentor (Special O. Henry Number), XI (1923).

Moyle, Seth, *My Friend O. Henry*. New York, 1914.

Nolan, Jeannette C., *O. Henry: the Story of William Sydney Porter*. New York, 1943.

Page, Arthur W., "Little Pictures of O. Henry" in *The Complete Works of O. Henry;* 1 vol. New York, 1928.

Pattee, Fred L., "The Short Story," *Cambridge History of American Literature*, II, 393-95. New York, 1917.

———, "O. Henry and the Handbooks," *The Development of the American Short Story*. New York, 1923.

Patterson, Ethel L., "O. Henry and Me," *Everybody's*, XXX (1914), 205-10.

Porter, Margaret, "My O. Henry," *Mentor*, XI (1923), 17-20.

Porter, Sara Coleman, *Wind of Destiny*. New York, 1916.

Quinn, Arthur H., "The Journalists," *American Fiction*, pp. 545-49. New York, 1936.

Ratchford, Fannie E., "The Rolling Stone: the Life History of an O. Henry Rarity," *Colophon*, V: Part 17 (1934).

Raymond, Dora Neill, *Captain Lee Hall of Texas*. Norman, Oklahoma, 1940.

Rollins, Hyder E., "O. Henry's Texas Days," *The Bookman*, XI (1914), 154-65.

Sessions, Archibald, "Some Odds and Ends about O. Henry," *Ainslee's*, XLVIII (1921), 150.

Sinclair, Upton, *Bill Porter*. Pasadena, California, 1925.

Smith, C. Alphonso, "O. Henry—the Man and His Work," *Southern Literary Studies*. Chapel Hill, North Carolina, 1927.

Stratton, Florence, *Postscripts by O. Henry*. New York and London, 1923.

————, and Vincent Burke, *The White Plume*. Beaumont, Texas, 1931.

Travis, Edmunds, "O. Henry's Austin Years," *Bunker's Monthly*, I (1928), 495-508.

————, "O. Henry Enters the Shadows," *Bunker's Monthly*, I (1928), 669-684.

Wagnalls, Mabel, *Letters to Lithopolis, from O. Henry to Mabel Wagnalls*. New York, 1922.

Williams, William W., *The Quiet Lodger of Irving Place*. New York, 1936.

Wilson, Lollie C., *Hard to Forget: the Young O. Henry*. Los Angeles, 1939.

Woollcott, Alexander, "O. Henry, Playwright," *Golden Book*, XIX (1934), 570-76.

Index

153